Lasalle: The Hussar General

Antoine-Charles-Louis de Lasalle

Lasalle: The Hussar General
The Life & Times of Napoleon's Finest
Commander of Light Cavalry
1775-1809

ILLUSTRATED WITH PICTURES & MAPS

John H Lewis

Lasalle: The Hussar General
The Life & Times of Napoleon's Finest Commander of Light Cavalry
1775-1809
by John H Lewis

ILLUSTRATED WITH PICTURES & MAPS

FIRST EDITION

Leonaur is an imprint of Oakpast Ltd

The author, John H Lewis asserts his rights for copyright purposes
© 2018 Oakpast Ltd

ISBN: 978-1-78282-756-6 (hardcover)
ISBN: 978-1-78282-757-3 (softcover)

http://www.leonaur.com

Publisher's Notes

The views expressed in this book are not necessarily those of the publisher.

Dedication

This book is dedicated first, of course, to Patsie without whom nothing is possible.

Secondly, to Sylvia who commits herself into these projects with inspirational conviction.

Finally, to Simon Bull who not only picked up the snowball of an idea and began its journey down the mountain without giving me the time to change my mind about it, but was also so kind as to assess the 'final' version of the text. 'First to come and last to leave' so to speak!

★★★★★★

Like Topsy-it grow'd
—Harriet Beecher Stowe

Contents

Introduction by the Author	9
1. The Lasalle Phenomenon	21
2. The Early Years, 1775-1791	25
3. The French Revolution Period, 1791-1795	36
4. The Campaign in Italy, 1795-1796	46
5. The Battle of Rivoli, 14th-15th January, 1797	59
6. Lasalle in Italy, January 1797-November 1797	70
7. Thiébault's Account of Lasalle's Italian Adventures	80
8. The Egyptian Campaign, 1798	90
9. The Expedition to Upper Egypt, 1798-1799	106
10. The Captured Lasalle Letters from Egypt	118
11. The Expedition to Spain & Portugal, 1799-1803	126
12. Lasalle in Peacetime, 1803-1805	136
13. The War of the Fourth Coalition 1806-1807	145
14. Lasalle's Blunder & Redemption	156
15. Lasalle: General of Division, 1806-1808	164
16. War in the Iberian Peninsula, 1808	185
17. Lasalle in Spain, 1809	199
18. Lasalle Leaves Spain, 1809	206

19. The War of the Fifth Coalition	219
20. The Battle of Aspern-Essling, May 21st, 1809	224
21. The Battle of Wagram, 5th and 6th July, 1809	239
22. Lasalle Assessed by His Peers	254
23. Marbot's Assessment of Lasalle	259
24. The Hussar General Commemorated, 1809-1893	269
Appendix	276

Introduction by the Author

This book came into being quite simply because this publisher had received a number of requests over the last decade or so from readers who had regularly purchased Leonaur books concerning the history of the Napoleonic era to the effect that they should like to see a book describing the career of this exuberant cavalryman made available.

It is comparatively well known that this publisher tries to accede to those kinds of requests from its readership if it is a position to do so. It is also common knowledge that the bulk of the Leonaur catalogue is comprised of texts which have been republished. Indeed, the primary reason for the creation of this imprint was a desire among the directors to make available in modern editions, at accessible prices, the kind of books that hitherto they had seen referenced in bibliographies and which they knew, if they were available to purchase at all, would carry the healthy price tag that accompanies antiquarian books.

On the subject of Lasalle, the issue was more acute, since irrespective of the fame of this paragon of the French Napoleonic cavalry, there did not appear to be—so far as the team at Leonaur was aware—an available work in English to republish despite of their willingness to do so.

There are, of course, many works available in the French language on the subject of the First Empire of the French and a few concerning Lasalle in particular, but given the financial constraints which bear on small publishing houses its first recourse (when it came to transforming a French text into an English

Charge of the Light Cavalry under Lasalle

one) was to turn towards automatic translation programmes to discover how far these might carry the project towards a finished text acceptable for modern publication.

These considerations are subjective of course, but for reasons which will become apparent, despite hopefully trialling this methodology on several occasions on 19th century French texts, the outcome seemed to indicate (in the opinion of the Leonaur team) that considerably more work on the text would be required by a contemporary writer after the completion of an automatic translation before a book would be suitable for modern publication.

That task, bearing in mind the texts to be translated were up to 150 years and more old, simply seemed too great and expensive at the time and so, with some reluctance since the volume of material concerning the Napoleonic period that could be published in English but which remains solely in available French is considerable, these kinds of projects were placed on the 'back burner' until the 'right' time arrived.

Nevertheless, the notion of offering Napoleonic material translated from French sources always held an appeal and has never been abandoned. So, on the subject of Lasalle, the idea was formulated that perhaps a quite slim volume could be created by conventionally translating from the French language the writings of Charles-Antoine Thoumas, 1820-1893 (which amounts, one could say, to a long article on the subject of Lasalle which appeared in a book among other articles concerning the careers of several notable French cavalry officers of the Napoleonic age) and thereafter supporting the text with illustrations and maps which did not accompany the text originally. Half a loaf, as the French saying apparently goes, being better than no bread. At this point the reader has probably grasped that the concept for this book did not originate from the high ground of contemporary academic scholarship!

Anyway, based on the above foundations the work began, unravelled in its practicality almost immediately and this book is not an English translation of the Thoumas writings.

However, in the interests of disclosure, readers should note that the text follows the chronology of the Thoumas work and, indeed, touches upon almost all the themes contained therein. Since this is a work of biography that declaration is not in itself surprising. We were encouraged to follow the Thoumas lead since when his text was examined it was apparent that the author has been fairly thorough in his research of source material because it originates from a variety of different ones, frequently referenced throughout the piece.

So indisputably the foundation of this book is based squarely on the scholarship of Thoumas as regards Lasalle's career in terms—in most though not all cases—of matters which the current author has taken as statements of supportable fact. In short, this book could not have been written without the guiding scholarship of Thoumas for it is that which contributed the substance of the content concerning Lasalle personally contained within it. The Thoumas text did, however, contain some obvious gaps in information which it was thought would be interesting to readers and where I could find a solution to these omissions I have filled them from other sources. Issues which arose after the original publication of the Thoumas text, especially regarding how Lasalle has been commemorated, have been added in the appropriate places.

Where this book parts company from the Thoumas work is as follows. Obviously, it is considerably longer than the Thoumas text which is a fact that needs little elaboration on the subject of content and has been written afresh which as has already been explained was never the publisher's 'plan'. However, having produced a full translation and not wishing to waste, as it were, the effort and expenditure required to bring the undertaking to that point, the view was that the project should move ahead. Whilst taking absolutely nothing away from the indisputable value of the Thoumas text, the problematic issues that arose were immediately apparent and several.

The first was that the translation revealed (perhaps predictably, since much the same can be said of English texts originating from different historical periods) that the original French language text was of an archaic variety presumably commonplace in the middle of the 19th century, but quite difficult to read comfortably for a modern reader in English translation or indeed, possibly for modern French readers! This was compounded by the use of quite unfamiliar phrases and metaphors of which 'making a pearl of his master', 'ordered a charge with the hard foot' and 'they pursued them with a sword to his loins' are probably sufficient to give the reader some idea of the obstacles. The sense of these phrases is clear enough to those willing to consider them, but few people would expect to find them hindering a text intended for a modern English-speaking readership.

There were references to the France of the Napoleonic period by comparisons to the France of the time of the Second Empire which were occasionally obscure and, in any event, lacked relevance for the modern reader. Of course, the original text was written for a French audience at a time when some of the events described in the Lasalle narrative were little further in the past than WWII is today. There appeared to be an assumption on the part of Thoumas, probably made with some justification, that certain events would be so familiar to those readers that they required no further elaboration by him.

For example, there were few clear signposts in the Thoumas work as to when events significant to Lasalle's life and career actually took place from, for example, the French Revolution to the various wars defined by the coalitions of the enemy nations. Since these momentous events had direct bearing on what was happening to the principal character of this book it seemed essential to include them at the appropriate points in the narrative.

The text was, indeed, comprised of very many 'assumptions of knowledge' which extended to the casual referencing of personalities essential to the telling of Lasalle's story as though the reader would naturally know who they were and what role they might have played in it. It was apparent that some of those assumptions would probably be misplaced for a large proportion of a modern general readership. I have made that assumption from the perspective of one who has read practically all of the biographies and autobiographies of the soldiers of the First Empire which have been translated into the English language and, whilst I make no claims to be an academic, influential characters appear in this book about whom I confess I knew little or nothing.

So, I have given the reader some insights into the careers of these kinds of people especially when I have suspected they may otherwise have been little known to general readers. These are often soldiers who, whilst important officers, did not necessarily rise to the highest ranks which would have guaranteed their fame. I have not, however, applied this principle to more well-known characters such as the Marshals of France, for example. My own assumption is that anyone reading this kind of book is aware of who they were.

In introducing this information into the text, I have discovered that these illuminations have actually assisted clarification as they applied to Lasalle's career for my own benefit which has encouraged me to believe the exercise was worthwhile for subsequent readers.

All this taken into account, in any event one must recognise (as I have incrementally done in the limitation of my own expectations) that Thoumas was intentionally writing a short piece in its own right and that bore inevitably upon how much detailed information would be encompassed within it.

Furthermore, for this edition, the literary style of the Thoumas narrative tended to be decidedly romantic and perhaps this too was to be expected given the subject matter, the times they described, the times in which the article was written and the nationality of the author as that bears on the subject matter and its intended readership. Thoumas was given to much eulogising about his principal character even when he was behaving badly or even ruthlessly, sometimes to the point of implausibility. Modern readership, it was felt, expects more balance on the subject of human frailties.

Furthermore, as one 'has lived' with the personalities (both men and women) that populated Lasalle's life and world, one comes to the realisation that their attitudes and behaviour bear little resemblance to the moral compass and social morays of what many of us would consider to be normal or acceptable in modern western society. It is not for us to be judgemental on these subjects for they reside in history as facts. However, later writers appear to have glossed over the implications of some of these considerations when they possibly have the potential to illuminate aspects of Lasalle's life. Without doubt, in the attempt of some redress, speculation has been involved when those kinds of circumstances arise in the text, but I have felt this was legitimate since to perpetuate the making of 'no comment' rather left 'an elephant in the room' and I trust readers will agree with my motives if not necessarily with my conclusions or suggestions.

There was also no small amount hyperbole as regarded Lasalle's role in certain events and upon examination it was felt that also required some moderation. Whilst Lasalle was indisputably the central figure of this narrative, it does not follow that he was central to all the events in which he was involved, for example. Perhaps, we can expect nothing less of an author of his time in that Thoumas was 'partisan' on matters concerning France and the conduct of the French Army and its soldiers. In short whilst this book depends in substance on Thoumas scholarship as regards the person of Lasalle in an editorial sense it is somewhat more circumspect.

Obviously, I have had to make judgement calls on these issues. When I believed the foundation of an assertion was potentially inaccurate I have undertaken further research, but often I have applied 'common sense' to certain matters which have resulted in conclusions more believable and moderate than those from a voice given to adoration of its subject. If more learned students of the period find that I am in instances in error then indisputably those errors are my own and I apologise for them unreservedly. Nevertheless, I hope readers will be satisfied that I have gone some way to iron out most of these 'wrinkles' and

Antoine-Charles-Louis de Lasalle

yet retain a 'French' tone to the narrative because, of course, the dialogue within the book was always in the French language and the times portrayed from a French perspective when the sentiment and spirit of the cavalier was perfectly genuine.

Any reader familiar with the motion pictures of director, John Ford will recall at the end of 'The Man Who Shot Liberty Valance' is spoken, 'When the legend becomes fact, print the legend'. Presumably we can thank Willis Goldbeck or James Warner Bellah (who, to give him his due, was a superlative short story author) for that line since they wrote the script for the motion picture. The phrase encapsulates a sentiment which has endured without much encouragement from anyone since man has been inclined to make legends out of individuals of his own kind. Though I have excised the references in the main text, Thoumas was not immune to the temptation of legends when it came to Lasalle since he refers to him at one point as 'Homeric' which rather says it all.

Simply put, I have found that Thoumas has been quite diligent in his researching of source material, but has on occasions, when giving his own perspectives allowed his sentiments to drive some of his conclusions. This is noteworthy as regards Lasalle's time in Spain because today, as a consequence of the documentation available concerning the great wars of the 20th century, we have few illusions about the behaviour of invading troops in occupied countries or indeed the attitudes of those who have been occupied towards their occupiers.

I have read enough histories and 'recollections' of times gone by to accept the notion that everything contained within their pages cannot possibly be in all cases the unvarnished 'truth'. The problem with portraying legendary figures is that the number of anecdotes which attribute deeds and words to them increases in speed and mass in line with their increasing fame. Then other writers repeat those tales 'with advantages'. How many of these anecdotes (which naturally would not be anecdotes were they not entertaining) does one include in a biography? Thoumas has, once again been quite, but not exclusively, cautious in fa-

GENERAL LASALLE AT EASE

vouring those tales he can in some way attribute to source material or raising queries if he believed there was some doubt of the veracity of an account.

I have discovered there are certainly some 'bubbles' concerning Lasalle that have been popularly reported that require 'bursting'. If I have been able to find information that, despite its potential shortcomings, originated in the 19th century I have been persuaded to include them especially if a source material reference has accompanied it. If I have discovered modern texts that appear to have drawn their inspiration from other recent texts I have been far more careful about including them in this main text.

On the positive side, some useful references to Lasalle's adventures as witnessed by his friends and associates appear in the Thoumas text and are available in English translation, for the most part published by Leonaur, which has enabled more expansive first-hand accounts to be embraced into the text of this book.

It may be that in the fullness of time there will emerge a more in-depth biography of Lasalle in the English language than this one, brought into being by an author able to devote the time and dedication to the task especially as regards further original source material. I have felt the need, in cases of contradiction, to declare both (and sometimes more than two) versions. In all probability one can never be certain of an absolute fact on some of these issues and would need to resort to calculations of averages to make a claim of what would be most likely. I confess I have not undertaken that kind of exercise to any great extent. Similarly, my own additional research, for reasons of practicality, cannot be claimed to have been exhaustive.

In the meantime, with this book, readers are able to read more of the life and times of this remarkable cavalryman of the Napoleonic era than might otherwise be available in print in the English language and I hope they will entertained by it mindful of the motives and methodology that created it.

John H Lewis, 2018

1. The Lasalle Phenomenon

It has been suggested that there was a time when if ten officers of hussars and other cavalrymen were to be taken at random to enquire who they believed to be the most accomplished general of light cavalry, there is a significant probability that nine of them would answer this question with the name of Lasalle.

He is, indeed, the most popular among the names of those brilliant officers who, from 1792 to 1815 during the ages of revolution, consulate and empire, rode at the head of the French cavalry upon almost all the roads and battlefields of Europe during the Napoleonic epoch.

It is easy to understand why this might be so. Who, as a young French cavalry officer at this time, would not wish to follow the example of Lasalle as a role model? Here, after all was the ideal light cavalryman, promoted to colonel at twenty-three years old, a general at thirty and then killed in battle at the age of thirty-four, in the fullness of victory, at the apogee of the greatness and glory of the Imperial Army, without ever knowing the days of its decadence or decline. The answer to that question was 'very few of them', but whilst Lasalle's admirers could possibly be numbered in their thousands there were more sober military men who took a decidedly different, less adoring and more balanced view of the man and his career.

According to his admirers, Lasalle would be alternately the elegant hussar, irreproachable in his personal appearance, renowned for the quality of his horses and his equipage, dazzling in his military costume; the gallant seducer with whom the most beautiful women were dying to fall in love; the boisterous companion giving his nights over to pleasure and his days to the battle, gathering his officers around a bowl of punch before leading them to the charge, always with a pipe in his mouth, 'swearing like a pagan and drinking like a Templar'.

★★★★★★

'I saw General Lasalle there with his baggy mameluke trousers and the pipe "in his moustache"', writes a contemporary, Senator Roederer, after having met him in Burgos at the peak of his career during the war in Spain, in April, 1809 before Lasalle went to the Danube to take part in his final campaign.

★★★★★★

The personal eulogies (and there are many) continue in like manner. 'Lasalle: The brilliant cavalryman who, losing his sabre in the midst of the fray, jumped to the ground to pick it up and rushed upon his horse without ceasing to fight; the robust athlete recalling the heroes of Homer by the vigour of his arm; the lively leader who, followed by eighteen horsemen, overthrew a squadron, who, with half a squadron under his command, decided the victory at Rivoli and at the Pyramids, at the head of a brigade of hussars, took possession of a first-rate fortress; the clever vanguard officer, an emulator of Stengel who was the first of the great light cavalrymen of this period.'

★★★★★★

For those for whom the comparison to Stengel may not have immediate significance the following may illuminate the matter: Henri Stengel, though a Bavarian by birth, rapidly rose through the ranks to become colonel of the 1st Hussars in the French revolutionary army and eventually reached the rank of General of Division. He was mortally wounded at the Battle of Mondovi in April 1796, under Bonaparte's command, leading a charge against the Sardinian Army. Of him Napoleon said, 'He was adroit, intelligent and alert—a true general of outposts combining the qualities of youth with the experience of age'. It has been reasonably claimed that Lasalle was, in one respect, the same breed of multiple talented personality.

★★★★★★★

Thoumas tells us:

> With all the qualities that were required of the light cavalry officer of his day, foremost of which was courage and daring, Lasalle combined a lively intelligence with a cultivated mind. His nature was for the most part personable and by most accounts he found it easy to make both friends and admirers. On a more intimate level more than one woman in his romantic pursuits felt disposed to love him including, of course his own wife, in whom he found it has been claimed, the most enduring and charming of personalities among all his amorous conquests. Lasalle could therefore be described as essentially a contented man in the fullest sense because success had always crowned all his undertakings.

More soberly, Lasalle was a charming man—not in the broadest sense, but to those within his circle and the image and reputation of Lasalle the rake and hell-raiser gathered acolytes like moths to the flame with often the same destructive result. There is little doubt he was also impulsive, reckless, self-centred, ruthless and a dangerous man who revelled and indulged in the excesses of warfare. Lasalle was not a heroic figure because there is little evidence that he was mastering his fear or fighting for any more complicated reasons than that he loved war. This is not surprising for, as the son of a soldier he was cast for war, became a soldier as a child of 11 and was cast into war by the violence of his time and place before he was 17.

Nevertheless, Antoine Lasalle cut an indisputably attractive, glamorous and romantic figure: an appealing likeable rogue, often displaying an almost childlike immaturity though possessed of a lethally sharp edge to his character which perhaps, is as good a definition of an anti-hero as one may imagine. Professionally, when he was inclined to be professional, he was simply the master of his craft.

Let us follow him—in chapters divided by the most significant episodes of his life—through his short but brilliant career as one of the foremost cavaliers of France.

MODÈLE DE LA STATUE DESTINÉE AU PONT DE LA CONCORDE

2. The Early Years, 1775-1791

Antoine-Charles-Louis de Lasalle was born in the garrison city of Metz, in north-eastern France at the confluence of the rivers Moselle and Seille on 16th May, 1775, the son of a minor noble family originating in Lorraine. Metz lies close to the border of modern day Germany and the influence of its neighbour upon the city was pervasive. However, Lasalle was born a Frenchman and a subject of one of the most successful monarchies that Europe had known—the Bourbon Dynasty.

There had been, at the time of Lasalle's birth, a Bourbon on the throne of France since the ascension of Henry IV in 1589. By the 18th century Bourbons also ruled in Spain, Naples, Sicily and Parma. One year before Lasalle's birth the old king, Louis XV, known as 'Louis the Beloved', died at the age of 64 years and a new king, Louis XVI, just nineteen years old, came to the throne of France. He inherited a government mired in debt and a population already resentful of the power of absolute monarchs. He felt he was woefully out of his depth for the task before him, though longed for the affection of his people and was determined to be of benefit to them.

Louis XVI would end his life on the scaffold, still a young man of thirty-eight years old, when Lasalle was just eighteen years old, beheaded by the guillotine of a revolution which, for a period of time, would tear the *status quo* of European politics asunder. In the maelstrom that ensued those, who naturally assumed opportunities would be their own, were swept away in their thousands and those, by degrees, who could not have

ABRAHAM DE FABERT
Maréchal de France.

dreamed of influence, power or rank rose to occupy places in their nation and in history which could only be possible in times of cataclysmic upheaval. This, though few could countenance it at the time, was the world into which Antoine Lasalle was destined to become one of most renowned light cavalrymen of modern times in the service of one of the most renowned military commanders who had ever lived.

Lasalle was a great-nephew of Marshal Fabert, whose statue was erected on the Place d'Armes before the Guard House in Metz. Contemporary commentators claimed, 'It would have been sufficient to preserve to France this city so eminently French in spirit and heart, if he who was in charge of its defence would have been merely inspired by the words inscribed on the pedestal of the Fabert statue,' which reads:

> If, in order to prevent a place which, the king entrusted to me falling into the hands of the enemy, my person, my family, and my property should be put to a breach, I should not hesitate for a moment

★★★★★★

Abraham Fabert was a Marshal of France during the late 16th and early 17th centuries, an expert in siege craft and fortification, a progenitor of Vauban and so was qualified sufficiently to ensure he would never need to actually interpose his family and possessions into a breach. To his indisputable credit, Fabert was the first Marshal of France to rise from the ranks which, in his own time would have been so unusual as to be almost unthinkable. Even so no one would have imagined Fabert's success would herald in France an age when the son of an inn keeper could become a king and a minor Corsican nobleman would rise to become an emperor.

★★★★★★

Lasalle's father, Pierre Nicolas de Lasalle d'Augny was a Commissioning Officer in the Royal French Army and a recipient of a Knighthood of The Order of Saint Louis. This was an award presented to 'exceptional officers' of the Royal Army and

French Infantry Officer, 1786

is considered to be the predecessor of the award of the Legion of Honour of the Napoleonic era which, in fact, this medal very closely resembles in appearance.

Though he was born to be a soldier, according to a chronicle originating in Metz, Antoine Lasalle chiefly derived his adventurous and combative character, combined with his 'sympathetic and charming nature', from his mother. On balance, that appears to be a fair judgement since Pierre Lasalle seems to have provided the stability in the family. Perhaps unsurprisingly other chroniclers have taken precisely the opposite view claiming his father as his principal influence which, on the face of it, suggests that Lasalle had a balanced childhood by the standards of the day, under the care of both his parents.

However, as readers will discover in due course, this second view may depend upon to which 'father' the commentators on the subject were making reference. Given his heritage there was always a greater likelihood, all things being equal, that Lasalle would have a military career in the officer class which could not always been said of many of the men who achieved high rank in the revolutionary, consulate and empire periods several of whom came from quite humble backgrounds.

In France, there were 23 commissioners (essentially paymasters) like Lasalle senior, each with a sizeable salary of 8,000 *livres* which was double that of a regimental colonel's salary of the period. Their functions, defined by the ordinance of 17th March, 1788, were of the greatest importance, as may be imagined, for the efficient functioning of the army.

★★★★★★

Madame de Lasalle, his mother, formerly Suzanne Dupuy de la Garde, was apparently regarded as one of the 'most handsome and most amiable' women of Metz in her time. Some references cite Madame Lasalle's maiden name as 'de la Gaule'. However, her father was Antoine Dupuy de la Garde who was, in fact, Antoine Lasalle's godfather and therefore after whom we may assume our principal character was named. Antoine Dupuy de la Garde was also a military commissioner and so a colleague of

French Line Cavalry, 1790s

Pierre Lasalle. We may assume the professional association between these two men led to friendship. Suzanne Lasalle was also undeniably, to say the least, high spirited as evidenced by the fact that she was once confined in a convent by 'letter of seal' at the request of her husband, after she had been involved in a duel with another lady of the town caused by (perhaps peculiarly for a married lady) 'a rivalry of love.' Rather than revealing himself to be a tyrant, the impression we have is that Pierre Lasalle habitually dealt with his wife's behaviour with a considerable amount of forbearance. This kind of action, which would be considered fairly extreme as a recourse taken against a spouse by modern standards, was apparently a well employed initiative for dealing with the wayward, since Madame de Lasalle later in turn confined her own daughter, Lasalle's sister, Marie Thérèse Suzanne, to the same convent. High spirits clearly were a family trait among the Lasalles.

The daughter eventually, upon her release from the custody of the nuns, went on to marry Monsieur de Garsault, who later became colonel of the Constitutional Guard of Louis XVI. The Constitutional Guard was a short-lived unit as it transpired which was swept up in the brutal chaos of the revolution by its proximity to the king. It was disbanded in late May 1792 and its original commander the Duc du Brissac was arrested on charges that amounted to treason and was subsequently killed in the 'September Massacres' of the same year.

Many years later having eventually risen in the army to become a colonel and subsequently a general, Lasalle was faithful in the attention he gave to his parents, to whom he served as a support from a position of little personal fortune. He always, as one might reasonably expect of a son, maintained a most especial tender attachment to his mother.

Thanks to the good fortune of his birth, Lasalle was an officer in the army at the age of just eleven years old which was by no means unusual in this period. In fact, he is reported to have been appointed to the infantry regiment of Alsace on June 19th, 1786, as a sub-lieutenant of replacement or substitute, that is to say,

French Line Cavalry, 1790s

second lieutenant of garrison in Strasbourg which had become a French city in 1681 after the conquest of Alsace by the armies of Louis XIV.

Of course, the politics of France were entering a period of flux as the influence of the Royalists declined and the various stages of radical civilian government began. So, taking into account the greater portion of Lasalles military career, especially as a cavalryman, one may claim that his actual appointment as an officer dates from May 25th, 1791, at which time he was classified as a *sous-lieutenant* in the 24th Cavalry Regiment. He may have held, at least by implication, the Royalist honorific title of *Mestre de Camp Général* which was a position of privilege, though with little actual practical authority, which usually allowed the holder to move rapidly to higher position in the army.

There were at that time, in each infantry regiment, two posts of substitute *sous-lieutenant*, destined for young men of the nobility who came to the regiment to learn the profession of arms and advance quickly. These appointments were suppressed in 1788 in the infantry but preserved in the cavalry. Perhaps Lasalle at that point and for this reason passed to the regiment of cavalry in which he was appointed sub-lieutenant in 1791.

★★★★★★

The 24th Regiment of Cavalry had occupied the third rank on the list of cavalry corps and was disbanded in December, 1790 by a decree of the National Assembly for taking part in the military revolt of Nancy with the regiments of infantry *du Roi* and *Châteauvieux*. This revolt known as 'The Nancy Affair' occurred two years before the final overthrow of the French monarchy though fully a year after the storming of the Bastille. That the mutiny occurred at all in the ranks of the Royalist Army was a clear indication of the growing influence of the revolutionary cause and principles in France among the population at large.

This cavalry regiment was subsequently reorganised as No. 24, under a new decree of January 6th, 1791, and under

F.̄ C.̄ A.̄ MARQUIS DE BOUILLÉ.

the supervision of the Marquis de Bouillé, governor of the provinces of Alsace and Franche-Comte. Bouillé decided to then recruit a certain number of young men from the nobility, and Lasalle, only sixteen years old, was admitted to the regiment among their number, no doubt thanks to the influence of his family.

★★★★★★

Although Bouillé was concerned with Lasalle only at the outset of his career, he is worthy of some further mention. It was Bouillé, in fact, who was responsible for leading the force which suppressed the revolt in the army at Nancy. The National Assembly approved of his actions, but certain radicals were critical of the severity of his response given that the sentiments of the dissidents were aligned with the spirit of the revolution. Bouillé was a committed Royalist to the extent that he was centrally involved in the plot to assist the Royal family to flee from Paris.

Following the failure of this attempt Bouillé was compelled to save his own life and he fled into exile, dying in London in 1800. However, his memory marches on to this day in the verses of the French National anthem, 'Le Marseillaise' in the 5th *stanza* as follows:

> But these bloodthirsty despots,
> But these accomplices of Bouillé.
> All these tigers who mercilessly rip their mother's breasts.

A harsh lasting legacy, perhaps, for a man whose principal failing appears to have been service and loyalty to the legitimate government of his nation.

No less unfortunate was Claude Joseph Rouget de Lisle, a French engineer officer, who wrote a 'War Song for the Army of the Rhine' (trans.) in 1792 which became known as 'Le Marseillaise' because of its adoption by the Provencal revolutionaries. In fact, de Lisle was a confirmed royalist, so was cashiered, imprisoned, came close to forfeiting his head during 'The Terror' and died in poverty, though he was awarded the Legion of Honour in 1831.

3. The French Revolution Period, 1791-1795

The storming of the Bastille in Paris in July, 1789 was the defining moment that history has taken as emblematic of the beginning of the French Revolution. Clearly, the disaffection among the population at large with the monarchy, aristocracy and the church had been fomenting for some time before the embers of revolt burst into the conflagration that resulted in regicide four years afterwards.

These events represented far more than a great upheaval in the affairs of France domestically and internationally for they would lead to a sweeping away of an ancient regime and its replacement with a new order. This philosophical ideal abolished the monarchy, proposed social change based, it was believed, upon freedoms for the common man and enlightenment and liberalism within a secular and democratic republic. The courses of human history tend to follow patterns and those apply to revolutions as to most other events. So it was that the hopes of a utopia were quickly dispelled by the repression of authoritarianism and militarism.

This great political metamorphosis would take the lives of many and disrupt the expectations of all. Some of the survivors who came through this period, by good fortune or strength of character, would ultimately benefit in position and wealth whilst others were destined to be utterly destroyed. However, irrespective of what the future held, it was irrefutable that the standards and rules of the past had been expunged and every French man or woman was faced, in the final decade of the 18th century, with a new personal reality: the 'subject' irrespective of his or her former standing had now become the 'citizen'.

Some of Lasalle's biographers say that he was then obliged to renounce his rank by the decree of the National Convention, which excluded the former nobles from holding positions as officers within the army. However, though this decree was repeatedly promoted by the most ardent petitions of radicals with particular revolutionary zeal, on August 20th and December 14th, 1793 and on February 27th, 1794, it was not actually formally voted upon until July 1794 (16 *thermidor an* II) Significantly, this came after the fall of Robespierre and so the adoption of the proposals contained within it were immediately suspended.

★★★★★★

Maximilien Robespierre was the revolutionary politician that posterity has held largely responsible for the revolution's worst excesses, most particularly the so called, 'Reign of Terror.' His politics, even among many revolutionaries, were extremely radical and his influence dominated the National Convention to the extent that many feared a voice of moderation would bring an accusation of treason with its inevitable fatal consequences. In effect, Robespierre became an authoritarian monster. He was ultimately accused of corruption, tried and subsequently executed upon the guillotine in late July 1794. Following his demise, the 'Thermidorian Reaction' ensured that extreme radicalism in the politics of the revolution in France was replaced by more comparatively liberal policies.

★★★★★★

The expulsions of nobles from the officer cadre were, therefore, partially instituted but not put into full effect as a general measure. Lasalle's resignation as an officer, on May 4th, 1792, coincided with the terrible events which marked the beginning of hostilities against Austria which had been brewing for some time on the northern frontier. A general sense of panic spread through the ranks of the nation's soldiers leading to outbursts of destabilising insubordination against their officers, many of whom were known to be members of the aristocratic families of France.

There followed the ignominious execution of two seemingly irreproachable senior officers both of whom had served the new government of France with distinction. General Armand Louis de Gontaut, Duc de Biron was guillotined in December, 1793 having been accused of 'lack of civic virtue' as an implication of actual treason. His wife was also guillotined in June 1794. Arthur Dillon, an English born aristocrat, who had inherited the command of a French regiment and who had demonstrated his fidelity fighting in two French wars was also guillotined in April, 1794 despite vigorous attempts to save him by his comrades and those who knew his worth and integrity.

All these events contributed to create a sense of instability for anyone in Lasalle's position within what were already volatile times in France. This was a period of palpable danger that held the potential for ruin at any moment which could originate from the least accusation and be followed by death for the individual and his or her family based upon the slightest pretext irrespective of who they were. In short, in France at this time no one was safe.

Lasalle undoubtedly gave his resignation as an officer under the influence of these events, either because he was compelled to do so, or, as Thoumas has speculated, because he wished to emigrate with his family to secure their own safety. If this latter course was indeed ever his intention he did not follow through with the plan for the young Lasalle engaged himself in the army as a private soldier thereby disguising his 'quality' as a nobleman since this consideration was his principal vulnerability.

Certain records indicate that Lasalle was a member of the 'Section of Pikes', a radical revolutionary group based around the Vendôme-Madeleine district in Paris during this period. Robespierre and the Marquis de Sade (who for Lasalle was 'Citizen Sade') were both, among other like-minded men, members at one time, so the young Lasalle was, to say the least, keeping

Chasseurs à Cheval, 1793

dangerous company.

To what degree Lasalle's involvement in the 'Section of Pikes' was a consequence of revolutionary conviction and zeal or an expedient for the sake of appearances and credentials for advancement it is difficult to judge at this point, though it is indisputable that this was a short and anomalous period in a life that had originated in nobility and rank and moved onwards following this hiatus (in keeping with the accelerated changing circumstances of these times in France) upwards to rank and nobility.

One may only speculate that living in the time of 'the Terror' it was wise to be pragmatic, calculating and as demonstrably unambiguous as to one's convictions and loyalties as possible. If that is the case then, assuredly, Lasalle was not the only young man of ambition in revolutionary France who was keeping his own council cloaked under the apparently levelling guise of the equality of citizenship for, among others, the future Emperor of the First Empire was, in his way, employing the same tactic.

According to his service record, Lasalle had been incorporated in the 23rd Chasseurs à Cheval on the 20th February, 1794, that is to say, nearly two years after his resignation. On the other hand, source records of service show Lasalle as being engaged in the campaigns of 1792, 1793 and 1794, whilst serving with the Army of the North which was created in late 1791. Records from this period are known to be notoriously unreliable and regularly contradictory.

★★★★★★

The enormity of the tide of revolution, which swept over France predictably shook other European nations to the core. It required little imagination on their part to believe that the proletariats of neighbouring states would be inspired to follow the example of the French people. Indeed, since the principles of the French Revolution were founded upon an ideology of equality and fraternity, those ideals should be intentionally applied and spread to other people's irrespective of national borders. Many radicals believed that it was the responsibility of revolutionaries to carry the class war abroad and that the army would be employed for that very purpose. Some of the general populations of other nations, before reality soured expectations, were prepared to welcome a French revolutionary army into their countries with the open arms of brotherhood as potential liberators. The reactions of the monarchies and aristocracies of European countries as heads fell in ever greater numbers into the baskets of the guillotines of France needs little elaboration. No one needed the foresight of an oracle to see what the future might imminently hold for them.

As early as 1791 the monarchies of Europe, outraged and certainly fearful of the spread of French revolutionary influence, contemplated intervention either to support the royalist cause or even to take advantage of the political instability in France. Despite its inexperience in the waging of warfare, the new power elite in the French Government, believing conflict was inevitable and imminent, took matters into their own hands and declared war on Austria and Prussia. The allies responded with an invasion, but were beaten by the French at the Battle of Valmy in September, 1792. This victory pivotally increased the confidence of the French Government and hastened the demise of monarchy in France.

The Army of the North was a notable force of the First French Republic and it fought with distinction and much unexpected success (certainly on the part of those who opposed it) against the First Coalition of Nations in the Low Countries.

Following the success at Valmy it marched as a significant part of Dumouriez's expedition into the Austrian Netherlands and fought the Battle of Jemappes on November 6th, 1792, which also resulted in a French victory. However, the good fortune of the revolutionary army under Dumouriez was reversed in March, 1793 when it was defeated by an Austrian Army at the Battle of Neerwinden east of Brussels. Dampierre, the commander of the army was killed at Raismes by a cannon ball in early May, 1793 and this disaster was followed by another defeat at Famars later in the month under Lamarche.

Chasseurs à Cheval, 1794

The tide turned in favour of the French at Hondshoote in September, though the general responsible for this victory, Houchard, was executed by his own government which did not feel he had followed up his advantages with enough expedition. French commanders of this period nervously knew that their government expected victories and dealt with defeated generals mercilessly. Jourdan won again at Wattignies in October of 1793 and not only kept his head literally and figuratively but went on to become a renowned Marshal of France under Napoleon.

The following year, during May of 1794 the Army of the North won yet again at Tourcoing under Souham and the right wing of the army under Jourdan, who was revealing his mettle as superb battlefield commander, triumphed again at the pivotal Battle of Fleurus in June. Very soon thereafter the allied position in Flanders all but collapsed which led to the loss of Belgium for the Austrians and the fall of the Dutch Republic. The Army of the North was thereafter involved in mopping up and siege operations until the end of October, 1795 when it officially ceased to exist.

Lasalle had, by this time, already left this army's ranks. There can be no doubt that these formative campaigns augured well for the new army and what was essentially a new nation. For Lasalle, given he was fortunate enough to survive them, they had demonstrably provided an essential foundation for his career on the fields of war. In gathering experience as a cavalryman, he had, by 1795, become well regarded, experienced, bold and worthy of following as a leader. Unfortunately for posterity, since these events occurred before Lasalle's rise to fame they are, so far as he is concerned in detail, largely lost in the mists of time and his early death, of course, precluded the writing of an autobiography which would have illuminated this period of his life.

★★★★★★

It is certain, however, that he committed himself to these campaigns on the same day that he had ceased to be an officer because, following the example of a large number of officers, he symbolically returned his officer's epaulettes to allay the suspicion that he had of simply stepped back to await a more favourable time to re-establish himself in his rank. Lasalle then sealed the matter of his conviction by simply volunteering and entering the ranks of the army in the manner of any recruit.

Military registries were held in the first years of the Republic with an extreme irregularity. M. le Duc d'Aumale, in his book *Institutions Militaires de la France,* quotes one of the most celebrated cavalry generals of the First Empire, who, as a volunteer in the latter months of 1791, returned home at the end of 1792 like many others, subsequently he was taken by the requisition, but without taking regard of his previous services, called *en masse* to serve in a regiment of infantry. He then subsequently joined a regiment of *chasseurs à cheval* into which he was incorporated and where he gained all his advances in rank.

It is, therefore, not surprising to find such an anomaly in Lasalle's service records. However, we have not been prevented from discovering with some certainty his movements following February 20th, 1794. Upon this day, as indicated, he was incorporated into the 23rd Chasseurs à Cheval, which had recently formed with the Legion of the Ardennes, a regiment principally comprised of troops from the German states who were ostensibly sympathetic to the objectives of the revolution.

Appointed *maréchal des logis* (a distinction of rank peculiar to cavalry regiments and meaning literally, 'marshal of lodgings' though equivalent to 'sergeant') on the 21st of March, 1794, he was soon renowned for an outstanding action in combat, especially for such a young man, which all his biographers consistently report. Tellingly, no mention of it appeared on his service records possibly, it has been suggested, because he had disguised his name when engaging in the regiment for the reasons already explained. Although most specific details of this action are not reported, he was credited with leading a cavalry charge at the head of several *chasseurs* of his company and seizing a battery of enemy cannon.

The commanding general of the Army of the North (probably the ill-fated Jean-Charles Pichegru who commanded the army from February to October of that year) called for him on this occasion, congratulated him for his courage, leadership and initiative and offered him the rank of lieutenant on the spot. Lasalle, however, refused the promotion, fearing, in all probability, that such an elevation would draw unwanted attention to his person and thus background by provoking the interest of the authorities of the revolution who may not be sympathetic to his irregular situation. Alternatively, it has been suggested that this promotion was refused on the grounds that Lasalle did not want to be separated from his men as an issue of comradeship or solidarity, though on balance subsequent events in his near future make that proposition improbable.

After the liberalising influences of the 'Thermidorian Reaction' in July 1794 (the effects of which have already been outlined) he no longer had reasons for hiding himself, and so at this point he accepted the rank of lieutenant without hesitation. This rank was definitely formally conferred on him on the 10th of March, 1795 when Lasalle was then not quite twenty years old though we may assume he took up his rank and responsibilities some time before this ratification since one of Lasalle's later promotion steps took five months between the award and its confirmation. Sparely built and just 5' 8" tall, Lasalle was ideally blessed with the weight and figure of an officer of light cavalry as if his destiny had been pre-ordained.

After this appointment, he remained for a short time serving with the 23rd Chasseurs à Cheval before embarking on the next stage of his remarkable career.

4. The Campaign in Italy, 1795-1796

Lasalle had, after a separation of five years, reconnected with General François Christophe Kellermann, who was renowned as the victor of the Battle of Valmy in 1791, where he had been instrumental in decisively defeating the Prussian Army under Brunswick. Kellermann, (the elder), who had been for a long time in garrison at Metz in the Legion of Conflans, was naturally well acquainted and on friendly terms with Lasalle's family. He consequently summoned the young cavalry officer to the Army of Italy whose command had just been placed under his authority, and by a decree of May 6, 1795, Lieutenant Lasalle was appointed *aide-de-camp* to the commanding general.

If Lasalle had really been the pupil of this general, it might be said that the pupil never resembled his master less notwithstanding the fact that Kellermann had delivered the revolution its first notable military battle honour. Kellermann may have been an outstanding soldier, but he was cold, methodical, economical almost to the point of parsimony, though on the positive side undoubtedly excellent in the training of troops, a master in the establishment and maintenance of discipline and demonstrably inspirational to the men under his command.

Kellermann (the elder), although formerly a major of hussars in the Legion of Conflans, had, according to Thoumas, little the gaiety and spontaneity of a brilliant officer of light cavalry about him. Readers may recognise that this regiment, which eventually became 'The Hussars of the Conflans', is the regimental name adopted by Sir Arthur Conan Doyle as the command of his indomitable comic hero of the Napoleonic light cavalry, the fictional Etienne Gerard. Conflans is also a name which had particular significance for Lasalle as the reader will subsequently discover.

Lasalle, however, was pleased to recount later in life that he owed what he had become to the old marshal. 'He gave me the first acquaintances of my profession; he taught me economics,' declared Lasalle on one occasion at the dinner table. Upon the recounting this ostensibly unlikely claim, everybody present expressed their astonishment because they all knew, of course, Lasalle was such a lavish character in all of his habits, but he added insistently—though no doubt mischievously:

> Yes! Economy! He always maintained you should not eat more than one chop for lunch. He would have beaten me with sticks had I eaten more, the good marshal! He had wished to make me a writer, and once he made me write sixty letters in one morning; I would not have succeeded in this profession without him.—*Souvenir, of Roederer*, quoted by Sainte-Beuve in *les Causeries du Lundi, tome VIII*. Incidentally, Kellerman was made an honorary Marshal of France in 1804 and Duke of Valmy in 1808.

Lasalle was soon disappointed to discover he had not entered a post which would bring him the action he craved. The task imposed on Kellermann by his superiors was, moreover, completely thankless, since his command of the armies of Italy and the Alps united, comprising 52,000 men was devoid of everything required to ensure it was operationally effective. Regardless these limited resources he was charged to keep the whole frontier from Mont Saint Bernard to Nice secure against a possible assault by an opposing Austro-Sardinian Army consisting of 150,000 troops. Remarkably when Kellerman was brought to action he consistently managed, despite his disadvantages, to fight a campaign consisting of a number of successful detailed actions, which brought out the best qualities of troops and his generals and which gave them beneficial experience for future conflicts.

Kellermann showed a characteristic great vigilance and prudence in the pursuit of his difficult task, but his young *aide-de-camp* found little occasion to throw himself into the dangers in which he could distinguish himself. Moreover, just at the promising moment when Kellermann was preparing to attempt the operation which led, under the leadership of his successor, to the victory of the Battle of Loano, November 1795, the command of the Army of Italy was withdrawn from him to be given to General Schérer. So, all that remained of Kellermann's command was the small Army of the Alps, scarcely 12,000 men in total, which rendered him all but powerless on the portion of the frontier he was limited to guard. This, as may be imagined, suited a young man of Lasalle's temperament very poorly and he became restless in his position on Kellermann's staff.

However, relief was at hand from the son of his disenchanted superior. François-Étienne Kellermann, (the younger), was also serving in the army and had become a member of the Army of Italy as *adjutant général* of the cavalry division. He, to Lasalle's delight, called his father's *aide-de-camp* to his side him to act as his deputy. This appointment, dated May 1796, decided the event filled future of Lasalle and for a moment, united two men who, together with Montbrun, are generally cited as the best cavalry generals of the *Grande Armée*. (See Marmont, *Esprit des Institutions Militaires*, and General Foy *Histoire de la guerre de la Peninsula, tome* 1.)

★★★★★★

This Kellermann was born, like Lasalle, in Metz and though he was not a flamboyant figure in the Lasalle model throughout his career he demonstrated his skill at commanding both light and heavy cavalry. Napoleon particularly remembered his brilliant management of dragoons at Marengo in 1800 which instantly elevated him from the rank of General of Brigade to General of Division. He served throughout the Napoleonic Wars and rejoined Napoleon during "The Hundred Days' where he commanded the III Cavalry Corps seeing action at Quatre Bras and at Waterloo where he is principally remembered as a commander of *cuirassiers*. Though wounded, he survived the campaign of 1815 though was naturally disgraced by the second restoration of the Bourbon monarchy. He died, 2nd Duke of Valmy, in 1835.

Louis-Pierre Montbrun who was also a highly regarded leader of light and heavy cavalry became a General of Division and fought with distinction at the Battle of Austerlitz and during the campaign in the Iberian Peninsula. He was killed commanding the II Cavalry Corps of the *Grande Armée* at the outset of the Battle of Borodino during the Russian Campaign. Struck by a ball in the side he exclaimed, 'Good shot!' before expiring.

★★★★★★

When Lasalle arrived at the Army of Italy, despite his recent appointment a disgruntled Schérer had already resigned his command, tired and frustrated by the constant stream of interference and orders to which he was subjected that came to him from the Directory in Paris. However, Schérer's decisive victory at Loano had given France access to the Italian peninsula. The young Napoleon Bonaparte, only twenty-seven years old, had assumed command of the army in Schérer's stead and had been in post for just two months. With that meteoric drive for which he would become famous he had by the time Lasalle joined his army already won the battles of Montenotte, 12th April, 1796, Mondovi, 21st April, 1796 and at Lodi, 10th May, 1796 where Bonaparte savaged the Austrian rear-guard.

The revolutionary armies of France had been fighting in the south following incursions by Austrian forces together with those from the Italian states including, Naples, Sardinia and Piedmont intended to take Nice and invade France *via* Provence. Despite Schérer's departure the Army of Italy was, by the standards of the day, in good condition and able to execute Bonaparte's plans effectively. His immediate victories put Piedmont out of the war

Lasalle conducted to Marshal Wurmser

and placed him in a position of advantage where he could give full attention to the Austrian Army.

The young newly appointed lieutenant lavishly praised his general who he felt was clearly a man of action and if not reckless after his own heart then certainly a soldier eager to take the fight to the enemy.

Lasalle said later:

> Where the Emperor was most grand was to the war of Italy. There he was a hero; now he is an emperor. In Italy, he had few fighting men and those he had were almost without arms. They were without bread, shoes, money, or administration. They could expect relief from no direction and there was anarchy in the government. He had few resources at his disposal, but a reputation of being a mathematician and a dreamer. He had not a friend to call his own and looked like a bear, because he was always alone with his thoughts. Everything had to be created; he created everything. That is where he was most admirable.—*Souvenirs de Roederer.*

Lasalle was now in the heart of the action in company with a general certain to deliver an ample supply of more action to follow and it was not long after his arrival in Italy that he began to make a reputation for himself. Matters did not begin, however, auspiciously for him.

On July 29th, 1796 he was with several other officers inside the town of Brescia which was at the time occupied by four French infantry companies and a squadron of *chasseurs à cheval*, when the Austrian column under General Quasdanowich marched in suddenly and seized the city.

Lasalle, at the moment when he expected to be at last in the centre of combat, was captured and now a prisoner of war. In due course Lasalle was conducted to the enemy's general-in-chief, the elderly Marshal Wurmser, who, 'struck by his young captive's open and intelligent countenance' was pleased to interrogate him, and asked him, in the course of their conversation, how old was Bonaparte, a newcomer to this war who at the first opportunity possible had placed himself by his actions at the level of the most celebrated of generals.

'The age of Scipio of Rome when he defeated Hannibal the Carthaginian,' replied the young officer, answering we are told by Thoumas, 'both proudly, skilfully and with a certain flattery, which, like almost all flatteries, charmed the one who was the object of it.' Presumably Wurmser was being cast in the role of Hannibal which, at its best was a stretch of the imagination and at its worst a blunt statement that, in Bonaparte, the Austrian commander had met his match.

That said, Dagobert Sigmund von Wurmser had an illustrious career as a soldier in the service of the Habsburg's to his credit. He fought with some success in the War of Bavarian Succession and Austro-Turkish War before the outbreak of the wars against Revolutionary France. It is not difficult to imagine that the field-marshal was drawn to Lasalle because Wurmser was a cavalryman at heart and, contrary to the depiction of him in the illustration in this book, he is regularly portrayed in the costume of a hussar. Possibly, in the young Lasalle he saw something of himself in days gone by. Between 1793 and 1796 he fought five battles through a period of constant campaigning that brought few rewards and much disappointment to him and his cause. At the time of his final battle he was 72 years old and worn out by his exertions. He died the following year, 1797, in Vienna. If he was not a general in the manner of Bonaparte at this time then none may berate him on that score for Wurmser was an indisputably gallant old warrior and demonstrably not alone among his peers as regarded his fortunes in the campaign in Italy.

Lasalle, following this memorable encounter was fortunate to be included in the first exchange of prisoners of war. Upon his release he was attached to Masséna's division, in which his usual duty, much to his satisfaction, was to command the advanced cavalry and so he was engaged in the work he loved the most. He was appointed captain on the 7th of November 1796, or, Thoumas asserts, rather he took the rank of captain without

LES UNIFORMES DU 1ᵉʳ EMPIRE
Le 1ᵉʳ Chasseurs à Cheval
2 — Chef d'escadron — Grande tenue — 1800

having been actually appointed to it by any higher authority, as was curiously, not uncommon at the time.

Thereafter he soon obtained the further step in rank to *chef d'escadron* (squadron commander) under circumstances described with a comparative (though potentially inaccurate) formality, which also dilutes the complexities of the full story, as follows on his service record:

> On the 17th of December, 1796, at Verona, with the Army of Italy, Captain Lasalle, at the head of 18 *chasseurs à cheval* of the 1st Régiment, charged 100 enemy hussars of Joseph's regiment, defeated them, and during the engagement, when surrounded alone by four enemy hussars, wounded all four of them, then crossed the Bacchiglione River by swimming, and rejoined his troop. As a result of this daring affair, General Bonaparte appointed him *chef d'escadron*.

Readers should note in the light of what follows that the River Bacchiglione referred to in the report does not in fact run through, or in the vicinity of, the city of Verona, which sits instead upon the River Adige. The Bacchiglione runs through the city of Vicenza some 30 miles distant.

General Thiébault recounts in his *Souvenirs*, in a much more romantic manner, a version of the action which earned Lasalle, to whom he was a close friend, this rank of *chef d'escadron*. It is included later in this book in Thiébault's own words. However, the tale that gave foundation of the commendation and promotion for Lasalle is as follows.

Whilst Masséna's division occupied Vicenza, the young captain had made the acquaintance of the Marchesa de Sali, an aristocratic lady renowned throughout Italy for her beauty and her wit. He had fallen in love with her, and she, on her part, had encouraged his infatuation 'with a violent passion'.

But their romance was fated to endure but a few days. The Austrians had come to occupy Vicenza, and an entire army interposed itself between the two lovers. Nevertheless, Lasalle, of course, wished to see the *marchesa* again. One evening, without warning anyone, he commanded 25 (18 according to the official record) *chasseurs*, the elite of the 1st Regiment of Chasseurs à Cheval to attend him. Collecting them at night, he stealthily crossed with them the line of vedette's, beyond the extent of the farthest forward outposts, and, by routes known to the French, gained the rear of the enemy's army.

The daring party arrived at midnight at Vicenza and there Lasalle hid his troops and went to find the Marquise de Sali. How that was achieved and what ensued thereafter may be left to the imagination. However, the lovers were recalled to harsh reality about two o'clock in the morning by the sound nearby of a pistol-shot. Lasalle hastily left the *marchesa's* side, ran from her chambers, jumped on horseback and galloped away to rejoin his escort.

The alert was now being given warning all to this precocious invasion and so the routes he had originally followed to visit his lover were no longer passable for a return journey to the French lines. Finding the best if not safest route he could discover, Lasalle's unit came across and charged thirty-six Austrian hussars (100 according the official record), who guarded a bridge (presumably over the River Bacchiglione which puts into question whether any swimming was actually involved). In the course of the altercation the daring little command took nine horses as prizes, then continued its way to safe territory by roundabout ways designed to confuse any pursuers.

When Lasalle came upon a German contingent in cantonments which he could not avoid he charged through the camp, bursting through its outposts by force and then dashed pell-mell over the no-man's land between the opposing lines. Finally, he and his troop of adventurers exultantly rejoined the French Army and regained his starting point without losing a man during the exploit. Other accounts say Lasalle lost four of his men in this adventure.

As it transpired, according to the accounts, Lasalle arrived back with the French Army at the moment when Bonaparte passed in front of Verbenna to review the Augereau and Masséna divisions. Lasalle, who was renowned for the quality of his horses and his uniforms, presented himself before the generals in a most uncharacteristic and untidy fashion, mounted on a clearly recently stolen Austrian horse which was still provided with its original harness including a rope halter.

He was questioned by the great man where he had found the horse, since it was apparent to all that something irregular lay behind Lasalle's unusual appearance.

'In Vicenza,' replied Lasalle, 'from whence I have just lately come.'

Undoubtedly this answer would have elicited the response from Bonaparte that Lasalle would have expected and so this was a risky though characteristically bold and calculated manner in which to draw attention to himself. It was, however, successful. Whilst the anecdote is a well-documented one it is implausible that Lasalle, of all people, would have been seen by Bonaparte unless he wanted to be seen barring the most bizarre coincidences which, had they been the case, would have embellished the account.

Having secured Bonaparte's attention he recounted his escapade without presumably touching on the motive which inspired him, but as if he had been inside occupied Vicenza instead on a purely military mission to reconnoitre the dispositions of the enemy army. Strictly speaking, according to Thoumas, Lasalle was still in the wrong, because an officer does not have the right to make an acknowledgement of his own initiative. However, as amorous as his principal mission clearly had been, he had apparently not lost sight of the responsibilities of his position as a *métier d'officier d'avant-garde*, and mindful of his duty in that regard he then reported on the positions of the Austrians in Vicenza he had observed providing essential intelligence by which the *général en chef* hastened to profit.

Bonaparte moreover, whilst he may not have been aware of the full detail of the young *chasseur's* adventures, was shrewd enough not to be taken in by an explanation solely concerned with duty from an officer like Lasalle. He loved to hear of exploits of mad bravery from his soldiers and expected his light cavalry officers, above all, to be the most careless of their personal safety. He was seldom to be disappointed in this respect by Lasalle and so instead of punishing him for a lapse in discipline, Bonaparte instead appointed him *chef d'escadron* in the 7th Regiment of Hussars sometimes known (according to Thoumas) as the Hussards de Lamothe.

★★★★★★

This regiment had been formed in the Vendée with squadrons detached from the 8th Regiment of Hussars, it had taken the number 7 at the reorganisation in 1794 (Curély's *manuscrit*). Other sources have this conversion on June 1793. This had occurred as a consequence of the defection of the 4th Regiment of Hussars to the counter revolutionary *Armée des Émigrés*. It later became (according to Thoumas) the 25th Regiment of Dragoons. Other references say it was known as 'The Hussars of Liberty' and 'The Hussars of Paris'. There is not necessarily a right or wrong in this information. Another of Lasalle's regiments later in his career, the 10th Hussars, was also known by no less than four other titles. On the subject of the conversion to dragoons other sources (including Desvernois, who served in the 7th Hussars and survived to write his recollections,) say that it was converted to the 28th Regiment of Dragoons. There was a 7th Hussars serving in the French Army during the Hundred Days which was then disbanded in 1815.

★★★★★★

This appointment to the 7th Hussars was provisionally made as described but was confirmed by the Directory on the 22nd of April, 1797. Lasalle was then twenty-two years old. Between his provisional appointment and his final confirmation of promotion, Lasalle once again notably distinguished himself on the 14th January, 1797, at The Battle of Rivoli, where he charged several times during the course of the battle.

Lasalle in action at Rivoli

5. The Battle of Rivoli, 14th-15th January, 1797

The Battle of Rivoli was regarded as one of Bonaparte's most comprehensive early victories since, during the pursuit that followed the battle a substantial proportion of the surviving Austrian Army was captured. However, at one point the battle itself was a 'near run thing' which had the potential to go badly for the French Army. Bonaparte had 23,000 men under his command whilst the Austrian Army under Alvinczi consisted of 28,000 men. The Austrians were committed to attack the French since the purpose of the engagement from their perspective was to effect the relief of The Siege of Mantua which had failed on three previous occasions.

As part of a two-pronged advance on Mantua, Alvinczi, in command of one element advanced down the valley of the River Adige. First contact with Joubert's small command forced the French to retreat. It was clear to Bonaparte that the main battle to decide the matter would be fought on the Rivoli plateau, the topography of which he was quite familiar. The typically complicated Austrian plan of attack consisted of six columns, which it was hoped would eventually envelope the French. On the left, one column under Vukassovich advanced down the left bank of the Adige. This column only managed to contribute some artillery fire to the battle.

Quasdanowich advanced down the Adige right bank with 9,000 men consisting principally of cavalry and artillery. Three columns in the centre under Libtay, Koblos and Ocksay advanced over rough mountain roads so had few artillery pieces. The right column under Lusignan was sent on an unsuccessful flanking movement intended to bring them to the French rear which failed to the extent that this force did not make a significant contribution to the battle since it did not arrive in position until the battle was effectively over.

This simple description of the attack illuminates that the Austrians squandered their numerical advantage by breaking up the army into small units enabling them to be dealt with piecemeal by Bonaparte. The Austrian battle plan required each element to achieve its objective without compromise and thus work in concert with every other column effectively to achieve success. However, Bonaparte would have been in a perilous position had the battle gone against him given his retreat would have been blocked by this manoeuvre.

Whilst Austrian forces were advancing onto the plateau at the outset of the battle only Joubert's 10,000 men, which were, of course, heavily outnumbered were in position to oppose the enemy which they did by focussing their fire on the centre columns. Other French columns were moving in towards the engagement and fortunately, Masséna's division had by this point arrived on the field and its troops began to be incrementally filtered into the line. By 9.00 am the Austrians had turned the French left flank, but Masséna's arrival had managed to restore the situation.

The Austrian column under General Quasdanowich, on the right flank with nine battalions of infantry and thirteen squadrons of cavalry, attempted to climb up from the valley floor of the Adige onto the plateau. This move then threatened the French right and centre so in response this column was raked with cannister from a battery of 15 cannon with devastating effect, followed briskly by an attack by Joubert's light infantry, which concentrated on Quasdanowich's right flank. Berthier's cavalry then launched themselves into a highly effective counter-attack which forced the Austrians to retreat back up the Adige in chaos.

In this charge, Lasalle was first noticed (according to Thoumas whose reference was probably Thiers) for his ardour fighting beside Charles Leclerc. The impact of this charge threw the retreating Austrians into a panic as their escape route necessitated passing through the restriction of a narrow gorge. Fleeing Austrian dragoons collided with their own infantry and soon the gorge was a mass of tightly packed, completely disordered enemy troops with no thought but escape. Upon this wedge the French cavalry fell in fury. With just 26 men of the 22nd Chasseurs à Cheval Lasalle captured, it is said, an entire battalion of infantry and seized five enemy colours. Later in the day Lasalle led another charge, which added to his fame, at the head of a hundred or so hussars against the infantry of the Austrian General Ocksay upon the Trambasore Heights

★★★★★★

Charles Leclerc was married to one of Bonaparte's sisters, Pauline. He had a promising career as a General of Brigade during the revolutionary conflicts in Europe but was ill fated to be chosen to lead an expedition to Saint-Domingue (now The Dominican Republic) in the Caribbean to suppress an insurrection in which slaves had risen and formed a constitutional government under the leadership of Toussaint L'Ouverture. The island of Hispaniola was rampant with disease for which European medicine of the period had no remedy and mortality among troops operating in the region ran consistently high. Yellow Fever decimated Leclerc's force and he eventually fell victim to the disease himself and died in 1802.

★★★★★★

Thoumas makes a distinction between Lasalle and Leclerc as regarded the second notable charge at Rivoli. He appears to have obtained his information from Thiébault's memoir which states, 'I do not know if Leclerc was in the battle. In any case, to couple Lasalle with Leclerc is ridiculous'. He does not explain why that is the case, but perhaps confusingly adds, 'Lasalle was in Verona'. In other words, according to Thiébault, Lasalle was not on the field of Rivoli, which, is a baffling assertion at this point,

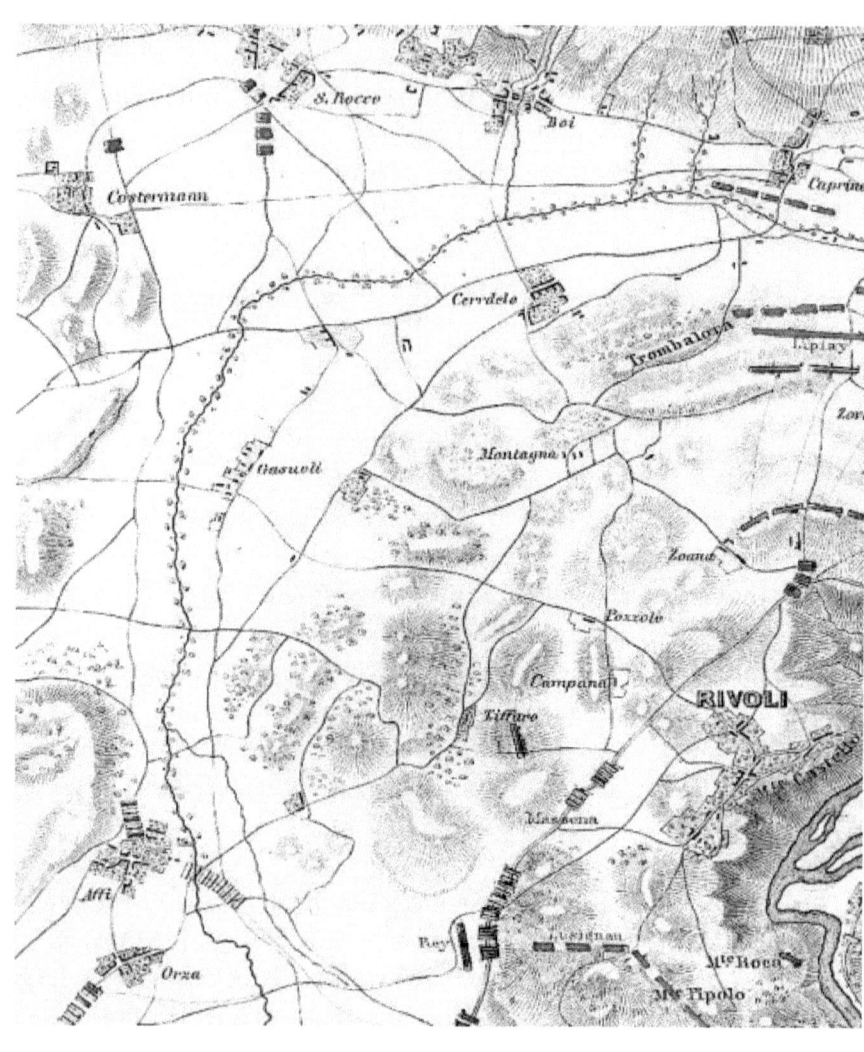

given the amount of source material otherwise on the subject.

To put Thiébault's assertion of Lassalle's absence in perspective following is an account from his memoirs concerning Rivoli where he was present and took part in an infantry charge with the 2nd battalion 32nd Infantry of the Line.

> I hastened to join the commander of the 2nd battalion, with whom I charged, while General Masséna, having Colonel Dupuy on his left, charged at the head of the 1st, all drums beating. It is needless to say the column composed of three Austrian battalions was overthrown and put to flight, that it lost one hundred prisoners, besides killed and wounded and left us masters of the position, which I retook. When the last Austrian had turned his back, I carried to General Bonaparte the advices which I had been ordered to give him. I may add that my conduct on that day was not unnoticed, and Burthe (André Burthe, *aide-de-camp* to Masséna) himself said so much about it that Lasalle and Rouvelet complimented me when I got back to Verona.

In fairness it is not evidence in itself that Lasalle had not been engaged at Rivoli because he was in the city after Thiébault returned to the Verona.

★★★★★★

Of this second notable charge which can be attributed to Lasalle's leadership at Rivoli, some authors say he actually led 150 hussars; Napoleon in his *Mémoirs* says: '100 cavalrymen.' The fact cited in Lasalle's service records shows in any case that he was for a moment at the head of a single squadron of cavalry, which despite any disparity in numbers reveals the charging Frenchmen were a comparatively small number in comparison to those who opposed them.

★★★★★★

Napoleon in his *Mémoirs* says concerning Berthier's charge upon Quasdanowich's column:

> The intrepidity of this charge, decided upon success; the

BONAPARTE AT THE BATTLE OF RIVOLI

This detail of the famous painting by the French artist, Henri Philippoteaux (1815-84) is interesting in its representation of the terrain visible in the background, but also for the excellent depiction of light cavalry uniforms of the period. The figure of the cavalryman on the far right of the painting presenting a captured standard to Bonaparte, given the famous exploit concerning Lasalle and the Austrian standards at Rivoli, surely may be intended to be Lasalle himself.

enemy was overthrown in the ravine; all that had debouched, infantry, cavalry, artillery, was taken.

Very little detail concerning General Ocksay appears in chronicles of the period except that it is noteworthy that references to his actions are usually concerning his indecision or poor judgement; neither of which would be destined to deliver good outcomes for his command in the vicinity of Lasalle or his commander-in-chief.

The citation in Lasalle's service record pertaining to his performance at the Battle of Rivoli is as follows:

> At Rivoli, he charged with twenty-six *chasseurs* the enemy Deutschmeister Battalion (so named since its first colonel was a Duke of Bavaria and '*Hochmeister*' (grand master) of the Teutonic Order), who were established on the plateau and captured it entirely.

It is said that in the evening, Lasalle, pale and tired, stood before the *général en chef* beside the flags he had taken from the enemy,

Bonaparte reportedly said to him on this occasion,

> 'Lie down on them, for you have well deserved it.'

Bonaparte had consistently proved his military genius since he had assumed command and by the time of the key victory of the Battle of Rivoli, 14-15th January, 1797 the Austrian Army, from a strategic perspective, was all but conclusively beaten. The Austrians had been prevented from relieving the Siege of Mantua and the immediate outcome placed northern Italy in the hands of the French.

A few years afterwards, in 1803, at a dinner given in Saint-Omer, the First Consul (as Napoleon was at the time) said in front of all the officers of the division of Bourcier's Dragoons:

> It is Masséna, Joubert, Lasalle, and I, who have won the Battle of Rivoli.—Général Roguet, *Souvenir militaires*, tome 1.

The Battle of Rivoli

François Bourcier was a well-regarded General of Division of cavalry, most notably of dragoons. He had the good fortune to survive the disastrous Russian Campaign by avoiding the deprivations of the retreat. He had been ordered to Prussia on an organisational commission for the cavalry. He was decorated during the First Restoration of the Bourbon Monarchy but retired from the French Army in 1816.

Charge of the Hussars, 1797

6. Lasalle in Italy, January 1797–November 1797

From the Battle of Rivoli until the end of the campaign, most of the engagements launched by the French Army against their Austrian enemy provided an opportunity for Lasalle to influentially distinguish himself. From Thiébault's memoirs, we have an account of an action which took place on the 13th of January, 1797. Thiébault accompanied Lasalle on this 'pretended reconnaissance' so we can assume the accuracy of the content of his recollections with some degree of confidence.

> On January 7, 1797, a general movement took place in the enemy's forces; he concentrated at Este, Montebello, and Alà. A large force of artillery followed his columns, and one hundred pontoons arrived at Treviso. During the 8th January Masséna got news of this through the friends of some patriots, the reports of spies, and the statements of numerous deserters.
> On the 9th, 10th, and 11th successive reconnaissances started for Zevio, Lugo, La Chiusa, and Caldiero. On the 12th, at daybreak, an attack of the enemy on San Michele was successfully repulsed; but on the same day the division was forced to retire before Alvinczi's troops and evacuate La Corona.
> On the 13th the commander-in-chief arrived at Verona, and this day passed in demonstrations. About four o'clock Lasalle received orders to march towards Caldiero with

one hundred cavalry and a field-piece, and to exchange a few shots with the enemy, in order, it was said, to find out how he would take it, but really to deceive him as to the movements which were to be effected that night. I joined Lasalle on this pretended reconnaissance. Four squads were formed, the gun being placed between the first and the second, and in this order, we followed the high road to Caldiero.

On our approach the enemy showed some troops, part of which, preceded by cavalry scouts, blocked the road in column. When we had got a good range, our leading squad uncovered the gun, which opened at once. Three guns from the enemy answered, and as all this could lead to no result, and, besides, it was getting dark and we had fully carried out our orders, we withdrew with a loss of one corporal taken prisoner, one dragoon wounded, one gunner killed, and the captain commanding the squadron with his right hand taken off at the wrist by a cannon-shot.

Thiébault has left us another superb account, which he witnessed with his own eyes, of Lasalle in action at this time.

> All the world knows the incoherent and inopportune character of the plans of campaign with which the Directory had overwhelmed General Bonaparte; also the way in which the giant had responded to the conceptions of the pygmies, who, finding Milan and Naples only a foot apart on their maps, calculated the distance by compass instead of by the soldier's pace, and took no account of the circumstances which most often decide the right moment for operations.
>
> It was, however, none the less true that Tuscany had to be subjugated and Leghorn closed to the English; the Pope chastised for the murder of Basville, and for the anathema launched against France; Naples impressed; fresh subsidies secured as soon as possible; while to get peace, we must

dictate it at Vienna. But it was no less evident that we could not dream of leaving Italy 'till Mantua was taken, nor march upon Vienna 'till the Armies of the Rhine could resume the offensive and keep the Austrian forces in Germany employed.

Further, even if it needed only three weeks to establish peace with Rome and Florence, while Naples had just concluded a kind of treaty, we could only attend to this in the interval between the defeat of one Austrian army and the arrival of another. The victories of Rivoli and La Favorita had made the surrender of Mantua certain, while the march of the fourth Austrian Army allowed barely the necessary time for an expedition against Florence and Rome. This was at once resolved upon and set on foot.

As soon as it was known that we were about to tap the wealthy countries of Tuscany and Romagna, Masséna and Augereau immediately and simultaneously claimed the lucrative honour of being entrusted with the operation. It became quite a subject of contention, the troops on either side wishing it to fall to their respective chiefs, and we of Masséna's army were preaching his incontestable claims to preference when we heard that General Bonaparte, on the precedent of the judge and the suitors, had decided to take the job himself.

On the day when Mantua capitulated, and Bonaparte crossed the Po—that is, February 2—Joubert's division left Rivoli and marched on Trento; Masséna's and Guieu's divisions also advanced, the former to Montebello, and thence to Vicenza, where Lasalle presented me to his *marchesa*. On the 6th we marched on Bassano. The enemy had covered it with redoubts, but we vigorously and quickly carried it. In spite of the terrible weather, the enemy was pursued and overtaken in the evening at Carpeneto. The bridge over the Piave was carried at a rush with the bayonet; two guns and more than 1,000 prisoners, including thirty-two officers, falling into our hands.

From the 10th to the 18th (February) the division manoeuvred about its cantonments at Bassano, reconnoitring the course of the Brenta, extending its lines to Cismone and Primolano, and finally effecting, first a reconnaissance, then an attack, upon Feltre, when the enemy's rear-guard, all that we could get at, left in our hands a flag, 200 men, two guns, over 100 horses, and a good deal of forage.

On the 18th (February) I took an order to Lasalle to start at three o'clock the next morning with 100 *chasseurs* and make a reconnaissance in, I forget what direction.

He had just bought a map of the country on a fairly large scale. We unfolded this, and perceiving among the embellishments of the title two little bottles, on one of which was written "Piccoli" and on the other "Refosco," he said to me, "You may take your oath those are the names of two of the best wines of the country; so, we will begin our reconnaissance with the wines." And it was over a bottle of each that we discussed plans.

The pleasure of being with Lasalle decided me to accompany him. We were not lucky enough to find the enemy; but another reconnaissance of his reminds me of one of the feats of courage and madness which he was always performing, without troubling himself whether they were observed. My mention may help to save them from oblivion. (As, indeed, it has! JHL)

On the 28th (February) he was ordered to start next morning, before daylight, with twenty-five dragoons, go to Bosco di Montello, and thence to Ospedaletto. Having discharged the first part of his task, he went on to the latter place, where his horses were so tired that he decided to halt, in order to rest and bait (feed) them, and let his men refresh. He placed a vedette at the upper end of the village, and remaining himself on horseback, with one corporal, ordered his second in command and the rest of the detachment to dismount, bidding them get food and forage as quickly as might be.

Thus, the men were scattered when the vedette let himself be surprised and captured, and Lasalle found himself suddenly attacked by a whole squadron of Austrian hussars. Fortunately, the corporal who had stayed with him was, like Lasalle himself, an extraordinary man in point of courage, presence of mind, activity, and strength, and the two, like a couple of Cocles' (Horatius Cocles, Roman soldier—famous for the defence of Rome—see poem *Horatius at the Bridge* by Macaulay for relevance. JHL) taking counsel only of their own audacity, resolved to face a squadron all by themselves.

A cart, without horses, happened to be just in front of them, and this contracted the narrow street yet further. They dashed towards this just as the first hussar got passed it, and Lasalle knocked over the hussar as the corporal did the same by the horse. The next two who appeared were served in the same fashion, and when the bulk of the squadron came up the pile of slain men and horses formed an obstacle which helped the two heroes to prolong their resistance. This gave the officer time to return and aid the combatants, and when some dragoons followed the defence was assured. But no sooner did Lasalle find eight or nine men at his back than he hurled himself amid the assailants, his example inspiring his dragoons to such a point that he killed or captured nearly the whole of the hussars before him and recovered his own vedette.

The following days were employed in movements of which the object was to support the left of Augereau's division, commanded, during the absence of its chief, who had gone to Paris with the captured colours, by General Jean Joseph Guieu. By Masséna's orders, it was driving any Austrian corps that were still on the right bank of the Piave across that river. Masséna had left Bassano with his troops to see for himself how the operation was going on, and, while sending out strong reconnaissances to prevent the enemy from uniting his forces, he went to Sëlva, his advance-guard driving a few Austrian hussars out of Vimadella.

When about to enter Sëlva, General Masséna wished to know if these hussars had crossed the Piave, and if there were no other detachments of the enemy on the right bank. He directed me to take half a troop of dragoons and to go up along the river to Santa Mama, so as to communicate, at the same time, with Adjutant-General Kellermann, who had reached that point in his reconnaissance.

I had almost reached Santa Mama, and was about to descend a wooded slope which gave a view over the country, when I perceived, at about half a mile beyond the Piave, which flowed at my feet, the fire of some carbine-shots.

I halted. "It's our dragoons!" cried a man of my detachment, known to have excellent sight; my field-glass confirmed it. Just then sabres flashed, and the dragoons were charged by a much larger number of hussars. I was down the hill in a moment, and, followed by my men, dashed into the Piave, which, luckily, was fordable at that point. Reaching the left bank, I re-formed my squad without halting and went forward at a smart trot.

Five hundred paces from the bank I found Kellermann, alone; being on a horse which he could not manage, he had not ventured to come to close quarters with the enemy, but he told me that that 'madman Lasalle'—to use his own expression—had "let himself get bolted" (by his own horse) and was in a deuce of a fix. As may be supposed, I galloped, and soon made out Lasalle, who was cut off by the Austrians and being attacked by them but was defending himself energetically. Without help, however, he must have succumbed, but the scene changed on our approach. The Austrians disappeared, and Lasalle was able to re-form his squad.

I might, no doubt, have joined my men with his, and, though several of his were disabled, we might have charged the hussars and given a good account of them, but we were on the wrong side of the Piave without orders, or rather, contrary to orders, we were in the middle of the Austrian troops, nor did we know what we had on our flanks or even in our rear, nor yet where a charge might have taken us. Consequently, at two hundred paces from him I halted; he wheeled and trotted to get in the rear of me; but just as he was about to pass me, and as I was moving towards him, he flung himself on me and embraced me, exclaiming, "Eternal friendship!"

It is needless to say that we returned at once to the Piave and recrossed it. It was high time for, beside the 75 hussars who were following us at a distance, 150 others, coming up along the river to our left, were ready to cut off our retreat. They seemed, indeed, about to cross the river in their turn, but the musketry fire of our dragoons induced them to withdraw. Thus, ended that scuffle, which cost Lasalle two men, two horses, and several wounded. He got two sword-cuts himself, one on his pelisse, the other on the upper part of his glove, while his horse got a sword-cut on the nose and a bullet in the rump, which caused him to be named "Kugel".

The enemy did not get off so cheap, as our men always "gave point." That was the last day of fighting which Lasalle and I had together, for Kellermann and he left Masséna's division almost immediately afterwards and went to earn laurels at the Battle of the Tagliamento.

On the 12th of March, 1797, before the Masséna division, with a weak cavalry detachment, Lasalle once again crossed swords with the enemy's advanced guard and this occasion was called to the attention of the army.

Thoumas tell us that a few days later Lasalle entered Valvasone, on the right of the Tagliamento, at the head of sixteen men on guide (scouting) duty, attacked an enemy squadron of *Uhlans*, pursuing it from street to street as it retired before him and forced it to unceremoniously evacuate the town before hastily crossing the River Tagliamento. Without hesitation La-

GUIDE DRAGOONS OF ITALY

salle continued to pursue them, thus opening the way for the French Army to follow.

★★★★★★

These were Guide-Dragoons of the Army of Italy and not, as has been occasionally suggested concerning this period, from the actual regiment of Éclaireurs which was, an Imperial Guard unit, not created until December, 1813. The reader will have noted, in fact, a repeated reference to Lasalle's command as 'dragoons' through his account. Lasalle was wearing the costume of a 'hussar' since he received a cut on his pelisse.

★★★★★★★

After the signing of the treaty of Campo-Formio, 18th October 1797, which ended the War of the First Coalition and hostilities for at least the time being. Lasalle, now commanding a squadron of the 7th Hussars in the following months was serving in the garrisons of Mantua, Peschiera and Rome. It is suggested that at some point in this period Lasalle first met Joséphine, the wife of General Victor Leopold Berthier who became his mistress and wife. Preparations for the expedition to Egypt were now being made and Lasalle's regiment assigned to it for service.

The Marchesa de Sali, deeply affected by this impending departure, entreated her lover not to abandon her, threatening that she would not survive such a separation and offering him all her fortune if he would remain in Italy with her. It is difficult after this period in time to conclusively say how much genuine feeling Lasalle had for the *marchesa* and how much of his affair with this married lady was simply one more amorous conquest; the dalliance of a dashing young cavalryman who believed his purpose was conquest upon the fields of war interspersed with conquests of the *boudoir*. One can also not know just how seriously Lasalle took the threat of suicide. There can be little doubt that Lasalle, a young man just 23 years old and a rising star of the light cavalry loved the notion of military adventure and glory far too much to accept or even consider such an offer from any woman under any circumstances.

A few days after he had said goodbye to his mistress, he returned to see her again one more time before he left Italy. On his arrival he found her husband, the Marchese de Sali weeping and embracing the body of the *marchesa* who had just died by poison, having apparently carried out the threat she had made. The husband confronted the lover, a pair of duelling pistols in his hands. Lasalle was clearly appalled by this tragedy, but with coolness, took one of these weapons, uncovered his chest and declared, 'I have offended you—you shoot first'.

'I would kill you, but that would not bring me back my wife,' exclaimed the *marchese*, and he went away in despair, throwing his pistol to the ground. (Bégin, *Biographie de la Moselle.*)

The above account based on information gathered from Lasalle's friends and family broadly follows the version of the entire affair in Thiébault's memoirs which is included hereafter for readers interest.

7. Thiébault's Account of Lasalle's Italian Adventures

Although this chapter requires the reader to temporarily go back in time from the perspective of Lasalle's career, it is included here since it contains an insightful recollection of this period of Lasalle's life from Thiébault's recollections which bears particularly on the escapade in Vincenza with his aristocratic Italian mistress which brought him to the attention of General Bonaparte. Given his close association with Lasalle, Thiébault's recollections and his judgements concerning his friend are judged to be in the main, balanced and reliable.

Paul Thiébault was born in Berlin in Prussia in 1769 since his father was a professor at the military academy in the city at the time. In keeping with most of his generation he was swept up in the tide of revolution and his early military career teetered on the edge of disaster as he was implicated in the accusations of treason levelled at Dumouriez. Fortunately, he was able to prove his innocence whilst Dumouriez only managed to save his head by absconding to the Austrians.

Thiébault served with the Army of the North and the Army of the Rhine during the Revolutionary Wars. By 1795 he was adjutant to General Solignac in the Army of Italy. He fought at Rivoli, Naples, Genoa and Austerlitz where he was wounded. In 1801 he was promoted to the general of brigade and general of division in 1808. He was present at the siege of Hamburg. Thiébault rallied to Napoleon during the 'Hundred Days' but did not fight at Waterloo, since he was given command of the defence of Paris. He died in Paris in 1846.

The following account is an extract from Thiébault's extensive memoirs.

> On the staff I made the acquaintance of Adjutant-General Kellermann, the brilliant victor at Marengo, and of his assistant Lasalle, a superb officer and first-rate man, glowing with cleverness and courage, full of talent, putting a charming grace into things which seemed least to admit of it,—a being, in truth, privileged by nature, who had no one there at all on a level with him and no intimates, and with whom I formed one of those friendships, which can be ended only by death.
> He was the son of Madame de Lasalle, wife of the paymaster of that name, and of "*Monsieur de Conflans*", as he used himself laughingly to admit. Never, indeed, was a son more like his father; he had his kind of wit, his kindness, courage, strength, his bounce, his grand manners, and his originality; he even said to me, in one of his effusive moments, that the selection of such a father for him was a greater obligation than the bringing him into the world. Mme de Lasalle, who was adored by her son, had been a splendid woman, and was not less remarkable for her wit than for her enthusiastic love for him. Famous for her gallantries, she was the subject of many anecdotes.

★★★★★★

Thiébault's report here seems to have Lasalle implicitly admitting to illegitimacy and naming a 'Monsieur de Conflans' as his biological father. We can have no way of knowing whether Lasalle was telling tall stories or if he knew this for a fact, though he claimed first-hand information. However, Lasalle is quoted as saying elsewhere, 'The choice of such a father is greater than my own obligations, than my own life'. It is quite clear from Thiébault's writings that he, at least, knew, who *'Monsieur de Conflans'* was specifically and appeared to know at first hand something of that person's character, but he has not elected to share that information with his readers and so with posterity.

At this point we can have no way, barring records of the period, to know the authenticity of such a statement though we can note its interest. The principal line of the actual de Conflans family held the title of the Marquis of Armentieres. Of the male members of that family who were living at around the time of Lasalle's birth, Louis de Conflans, Marquis of Armentières was a French general and Marshal of France who was born in 1711 but died in 1774. He fathered two sons, Louis Gabriel born 1735 and Louis Charles born 1737. How that may have influenced the life of Antoine Charles Louis de Lasalle born 1775, if at all, we may only speculate. For reasons that may have no bearing on this matter it may be acknowledged that Antoine Lasalle referred to himself by his second name as 'Charles'.

Of course, it may well be that Lasalle's code name for his father was simply that and had no bearing on the de Conflans family at all. However, at the risk of over analysing Lasalle's whimsical name for his father it did occur to the present writer that the younger brother of the holder of a title in France was sometimes known by the honorific, '*Monsieur*' as in the case of the brother of the king, for example. It should also be remembered that Kellerman (senior) served in the 'Conflans' regiment, lived in Metz, knew the Lasalle family well and became Antoine Lasalle's, mentor and patron. However, Thoumas' description of his personality hardly squares with that of Thiébault concerning Lasalle's actual father though both views are, of course, entirely subjective.

★★★★★★

Thiébault continued:

> When I joined the division, the fighting at Arcole (where, contrary to myth neither Bonaparte nor Augereau crossed the bridge) had taken place only a few days previously (17th November, 1796), more than a third of Alvinczi's army and a sixth of ours being disabled. In spite of this difference, equality was far from being established. Our position continued to be dangerous, but the enemy had been scared by the audacity and profundity shown in the

operations, which had snatched what he thought a certain victory out of his hands. His army was in no more condition to resume the offensive than was ours to attack; he needed rest and reinforcements, which we were awaiting equally, and the respite enabled us to receive them, and Bonaparte was not the man to fail to utilise it. He brought up at once all who were available in France or in the depots, looked after the wants of the troops, gave every corps new colours, and, finally, visited all the divisions, coming to Verona to review those of Masséna and Augereau.

Those two divisions, covered with glory, proud of their feats, and the first especially proud of its general, who already had the name of "the pet child of Victory," formed the largest force in the Army of Italy. It was for that reason that they had been united at Verona, whence they could aid Joubert and watch Tyrol, and, while threatening Vienna, were in a position to hold the Adige and cover the corps charged with the blockade of Mantua.

The review took place at the gates of Verona. Complete full-dress had been ordered, and the care taken to execute the order caused all the more surprise at the appearance of Lasalle, who, usually the most brilliant as he was the most handsome officer in the army, turned up in an old pelisse, pantaloons, and dirty boots, and riding an Austrian hussar's horse, on which he had been careful to leave its saddle, its bridle, and even its rope-halter.

The surprise caused by this get-up was universal, and the commander-in-chief's first question was:

"What horse have you got there?"

The answer was ready: "A horse I have just taken from the enemy!"

"Where?"

"At Vicenza, general," replied Lasalle

"Are you mad?" exclaimed the astounded Bonaparte.

"I have just come thence; indeed, I bring news from thence, which you will, perhaps, deem not unimportant."

Bonaparte at once took him aside, talked with him for a quarter of an hour, and came back to the group formed by Generals Berthier, Masséna and Augereau, and by the staff-officers present, announcing that he had just promoted Lasalle to the rank of 'major' *(chef d'escadron)*.

Here is the rest of the story.

Lasalle, who was a man of many accomplishments and a highly susceptible temperament, found, amid all his enthusiasm for his military duties, some time at his disposal for love-affairs. He was carrying on one of these with a Marchesa di Sale, one of the cleverest and most charming women of Upper Italy, who afterwards poisoned herself in despair at the loss of him. She lived at Vicenza, and the withdrawal of our army across the Adige had interrupted the liaison. The lovers had found means to correspond across the Austrian Army, but correspondence was not enough for Lasalle, and he resolved on one of those enterprises, which success alone will justify.

Selecting twenty-five men from the 1st Regiment of Cavalry (1st regiment of *Chasseurs à Cheval*—according to Thoumas who also quotes Lasalle's service record on the matter. JHL)—one of the best that we then had—he assembled them after nightfall and set out at once, without orders, without letting anyone know, without even a show of authority. He passed the enemy's vedettes unperceived, escaped his pickets, got through the hills to the rear of the Austrian Army, and, marching without cockades and with cloaks unfolded, by mountain roads which he knew, reached Vicenza, where he knew there was no full garrison, toward midnight, concealed his little troop, and hastened to the *marchesa*.

About half-past two in the morning, as he was preparing to be off, some pistol-shots were heard. He mounted at once and rejoined his escort, learning then that he had been discovered and surrounded. The most direct roads were strongly guarded, but he recollected one point which was likely still to be open and hastened thither. Thirty-six hussars were occupying it; he charged them without knowing their numbers, overturned them, captured and brought away nine horses; then he returned by a different road which involved a long way round, avoided cantonments, spoke German, and passed himself off for an Austrian to the men of a picket through which he had to pass. Lastly, marching as fast as possible, he fell upon the rear of the last Austrian advanced post, sabred all that he could get at, and returned by daylight to San Martino d'Albaro, whence he had started, without having lost a single man. But the fleeting moments, which Lasalle had passed at Vicenza were not devoted solely to making love. The *marchesa*, prepared for the interview, had procured some valuable information, which she had passed on to him. Moreover, he had chosen for his prank the night preceding the commander-in-chief's review. On his return he had avoided showing himself, so as not to have to report to anyone, and then had waited for the moment when, by appearing before Bonaparte in the get-up and on the horse which I have mentioned, he might make the most he could of an attempt which would have either to be punished or rewarded.

Whilst these accounts seem to deal with the affair conclusively, General Roguet, who had taken part in the Italian campaign as the *chef de bataillon* in Joubert's division, and who could almost pass for an eye-witness, gave the Marquise de Sali's suicide another motive.

He tells us:

When the news of the treaty of Campo Formio, spread abroad and the conditions contained within it were known, despair was seized upon by the Venetians, who had now to their horror become Austrian subjects. The first estate owning families emigrated to Cisalpine. Consternation

Officer of Hussars, 1797

was general throughout the population and several people of the higher class actually killed themselves. A young woman of Vicenza, of remarkable beauty, of great spirit and character above her sex, the Countess Sallé, the pride of one of the most considerable houses on the mainland could not bear what she regarded as a supreme humiliation. She poisoned herself in the presence of her grieving family, and died a few moments later in the most atrocious agony.—Roguet, *Souvenirs militaires tome* 1.

★★★★★★

We can only speculate which version of this tale is the most probable. The principal issue for Venetians, after all, was the fall of the Venetian Republic which had existed since 697 *A.D.* and had been brought to an end recently by the invading French. Some of the population embraced revolutionary ideals, but predictably these suited families of privilege the least. That having been said, Thiébault gives us the impression that much of the intelligence Lasalle obtained about enemy positions in Vicenza came not necessarily from his own observations, but from information provided to him by his lover at the times of their intimate liaisons. This, if true, speaks in measure to her patriotic convictions since one way or another she was colluding with 'the enemy' all be it against the interests of another enemy.

Whilst the terms of the treaty of Campo Formio were harsher than the conditions it replaced, the fact is that one occupation was being exchanged for another and the Venetians had already lost their liberty. Bonaparte had declared, 'I shall be an Attila to the state of Venice' which were not words of encouragement in anyone's language.

Indeed, the French were as loathed in Venice as any occupying army tends to be and they conducted themselves typically by looting the great artworks of the city and transporting them back to Paris. Among these treasures were the four magnificent Roman bronze, 'Horses of St. Mark' which famously stood on the portico of the Basilica of San Marco. The French used them in the design of the Arc de Triomphe du Carrousel. These stat-

Embarkation of the French Army to Egypt, Toulon

ues were originally looted from Constantinople where they had adorned the Hippodrome. Venice had them returned to the city in 1815 after the final fall of Napoleon.

In chronological order, the first Brigadier Gerard story is set in Venice and concerns both the theft of artworks and the assassinations of French soldiers and is worthy of reading for flavour of the period. Whilst these famous humorous tales are indisputably fiction, Sir Arthur Conan Doyle was an accomplished student of the Napoleonic era and his Gerard stories drew heavily on the memoirs of actual French soldiers; identifiable versions of their actual adventures regularly being woven into the Brigadier Gerard tales.

★★★★★★

So, whether Lasalle was actually the motivation, all be it unwittingly, of this young woman's death or not, there is no doubt he experienced extreme grief as a consequence of it. It is a hard thing for anyone, especially a young person, to imagine that one has been responsible for the death of someone with whom one has shared intimacies.

Nevertheless, he was young and excited at the prospect of the extraordinary combats offered in the forthcoming campaign in Egypt for he was bound for an exotic continent, so alien from Europe that it was almost beyond his imagining.

8. The Egyptian Campaign, 1798

Given the many and substantial obstacles that lay before revolutionary France during this period it may seem the proposal of the campaign in Egypt in 1798 was, to say the least, an ill-advised distraction. The idea behind it (which was not a recent one in France) was to defend and so promote French trade interests, routes and potentials by destabilising those of the British particularly as that applied to the Indian sub-continent.

There can be no doubt this proposal had its share of Gallic romance attached to it for accompanying the *L'Armée d'Orient* was a large scientific expedition comprised of *savants* (scientists and scholars) which, though anachronistic in a military expedition, ultimately, but also arguably, made the greatest contribution of the enterprise, especially as that concerned Egyptology. The 'Rosetta Stone' discovered by a French officer of engineers, Pierre-François Bouchard, during this expedition in July 1799, for example, later famously enabled Champollion to decipher the meanings of ancient Egyptian hieroglyphics.

As a military expedition, the Egyptian and Syrian Campaign was, however, poorly conceived and almost certainly destined from the outset to be a strategic *cul-de-sac*. The fighting cost the lives of many French soldiers, who would have better employed elsewhere on continental Europe, for the new French nation had enemies nearer to its borders than the Ottomans and more pressing problems to resolve than could be found in the south-eastern Mediterranean by coming to battle with the Royal Navy of the day which was unparalleled in the prosecution of naval warfare.

In August 1799, after an abortive absence, Bonaparte eventually discreetly quit Cairo, boarded a frigate and returned to France leaving his Egyptian Army to shift for itself, having achieved nothing of political benefit for France. It was the British who ended the matter through decisive actions at sea and on land, with the 'Battle of the Nile' under Nelson in August just weeks after the initial French landing and in the action at Alexandria in 1801 where the British Army under Abercromby concluded the business, though at the cost of the general's life.

Whilst Wellington and Blücher defeated Napoleon in the last moments of his final great gamble on a Belgian battlefield it was, in reality, the Royal Navy that consistently brought the machinations of the emperor to ruin. An island race will perforce bring forth great sailors where a continental nation will give rise to great soldiers. This unacceptable truth was a cause of perpetual vexation to Napoleon and Bonaparte had his first harsh lesson of the fact, courtesy of Nelson at 'The Battle of the Nile'. But that he had heeded its clarion warnings in all his dealings thereafter.

However, from the perspective of our principal character, it is perhaps during the fighting in Egypt that Lasalle earned the laurels which led to his name becoming legendary among light cavalrymen. We are told that Lasalle boarded ship, the frigate *La Courageuse* from the port of Civitavecchia in Italy in company with General Desaix. His regiment, the 7th Hussars was joined with the 20th Dragoons in Mireur's brigade.

★★★★★★

François Mireur was a brigadier-general by the time of the Egyptian Campaign and was twenty-eight years old. An experienced officer, he had fought through the battles of the revolution, including at Valmy and with distinction during the campaign in Italy which had earned him his promotion. Mireur's time in his new brigade was very short for on July 9th, 1798, just over a week after the landings of the French Army in Egypt, at Damanhur, he

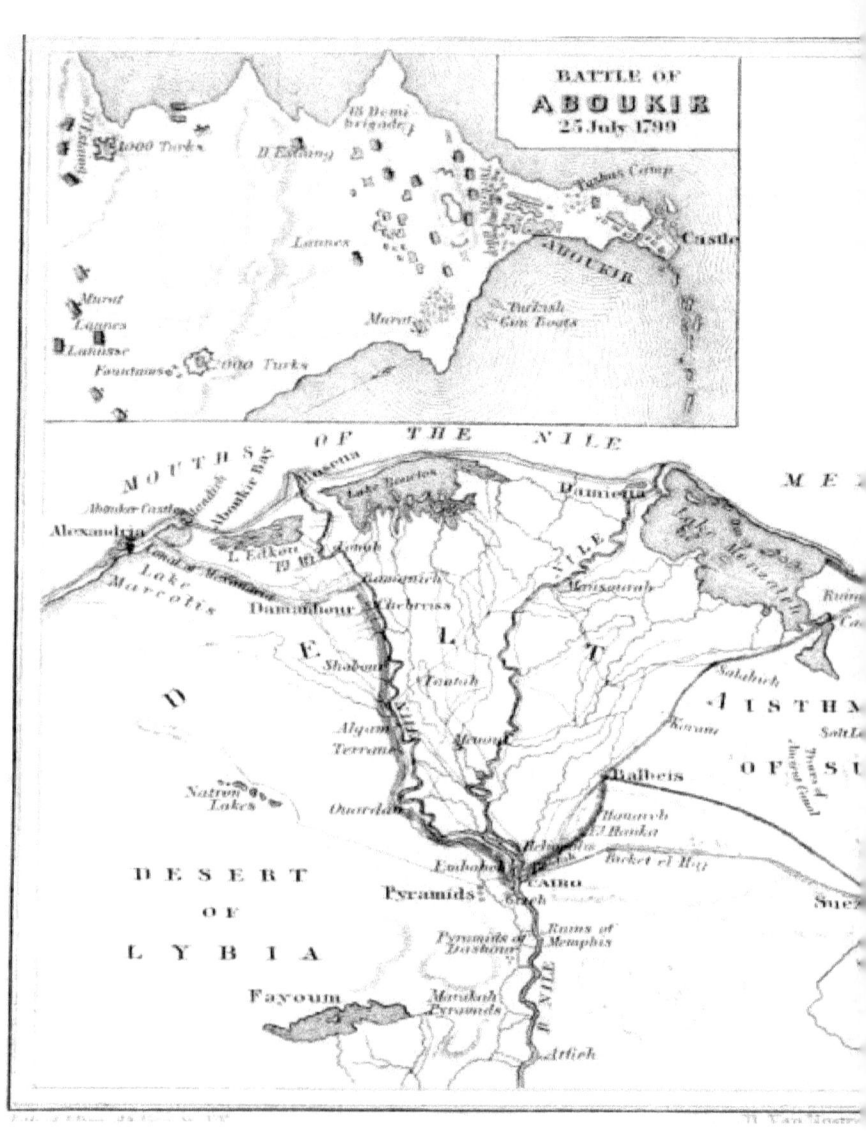

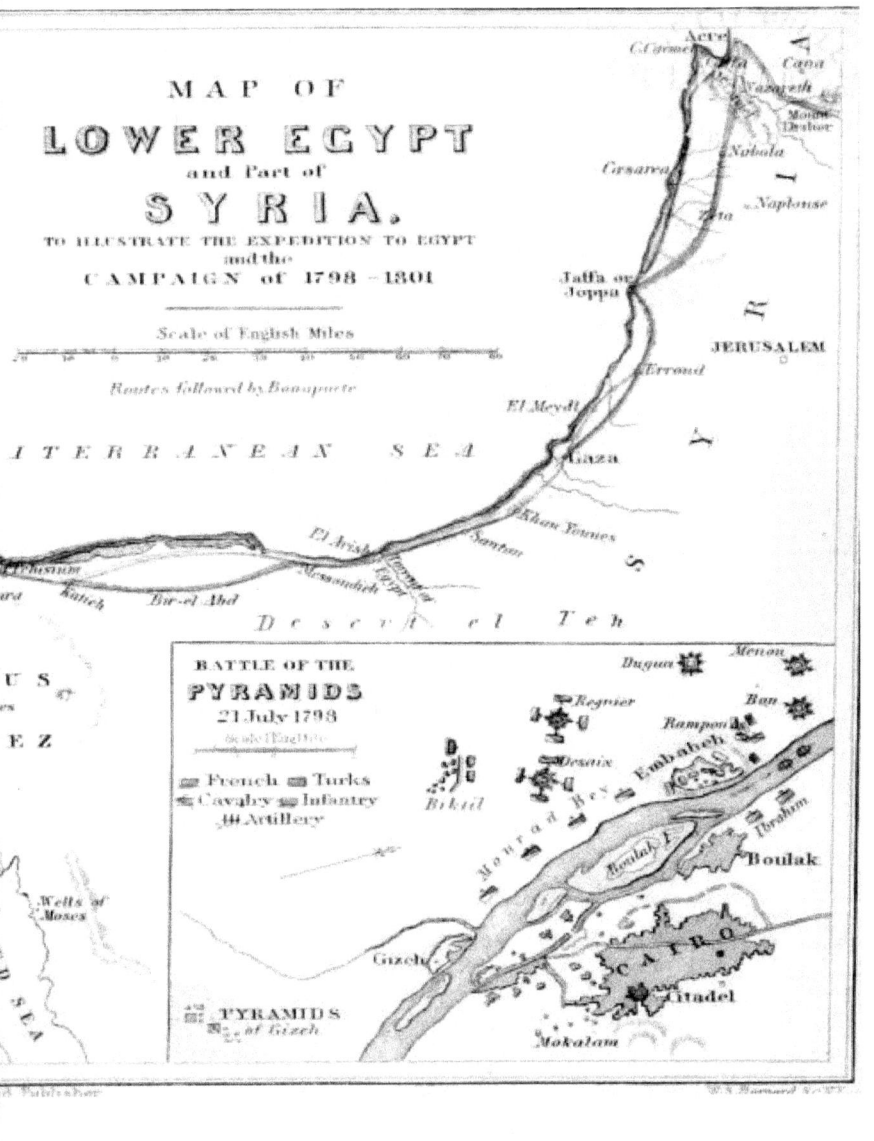

was killed. Hostile Arabs never ceased to harass the French line of march and presented a perpetual danger prowling around cantonments awaiting the opportunity to attack the unwary.

Mireur had recently purchased an Arab horse and wanted to leave the camp alone to try it. The outpost soldiers pleaded with him in vain against this obviously rash enterprise. Mireur mounted his horse and galloped towards a hill some 200 yards from the camp whereupon he was suddenly set upon by three Arabs who killed him with spears and stripped him, making their escape before the duty soldiers could come to his aid. The official report of the incident differs somewhat in that it states Mireur was travelling from one encampment to another at the time of his death.

★★★★★★

The French Army of 40,000 men, having made its presence felt on Malta, landed at Alexandria, and on July 1st, 1798 and soon thereafter brought about the first action of the campaign when it engaged a Mamluk (Mameluke) and Arab force of 4,000 at Chebriess, killing 600 of them. Bonaparte marched on Cairo driving the fleeing enemy before him. On July 21st Bonaparte, at the head of 25,000 men (other references state 20,000) having left reserves and garrisons in his rear, arrived before the village of Embabe (Embabeh), nine miles from the Pyramids of Giza and four miles from Cairo. The heat was typically excessive and the troops exhausted, but there was little time for recuperation or delay for the enemy host was at hand.

As Bonaparte drew up his battle lines he allegedly pointed out the tips of the pyramids in the distance to his men which lay beyond the enemy battle lines. Later this occurrence was transformed into a grand eloquent speech but, according to later historians, the Pyramids are not apparently visible from the battlefield, though this writer can attest that, even in modern times, they are a feature in the landscape practically everywhere on this side of Cairo. Whatever the truth of the matter, the ensuing con-

MAMELUKE IN FULL ARMOUR

flict was named 'The Battle of the Pyramids' as it was, perhaps, always destined to be, for who would, given the free choice as the victor, call it anything other?

★★★★★★

The Mamluks (the word can be spelled, incidentally, in seven different ways and in any event the plural of Mamluk—meaning 'property' is correctly Mamalik) were Muslim slave soldiers and ultimately Muslim rulers of slave origin. They existed from the 9th to the 19th centuries and were influential from Iraq through Syria to Egypt. In 1768 The Egyptian Mamluks declared independence from their Turkish Ottoman masters but were defeated and remained vassals. Interestingly, during 1799, the French general, Kléber had formed a mounted company of Mamluks. These men were the foundation of the small unit that became the Mamelukes of the Imperial Guard.
After the defeat of the French in Egypt the Mamluks took advantage of civil unrest in Cairo in 1805 and attempted to seize power. They defeated Turkish forces on several occasions but were unable to consolidate their rule. In 1811, the Egyptian governor, Muhammad Ali, came to the realisation that the country would remain unstable so long as the Mamluks retained feudal authority and that they had to be eradicated. The ensuing slaughter accounted for many of the Mamluk families but some fled to Sudan where they were finally defeated in 1820.

★★★★★★

The enemy force consisted of over 60,000 effectives, though the engaged number has been estimated at 21,000 (other references state 25,000) some of the total being in position on the other side of the River Nile. Bonaparte formed his entire army into enormous defensive divisional squares with the cavalry and baggage protected in their centres and cannon at their corners upon which the Mamluk cavalry, on which the enemy was heavily reliant, dashed itself in vain and were slaughtered.

The French divisions advanced south in echelon, right flank

leading and left covered by the River Nile. Estimates on losses vary wildly but conservatively, the French lost 300 men (of which less than 30 were allegedly killed) whilst at least 6,000 Mamluks and others perished. Not for the first time (or the last) an army whose practices were rooted in the past and founded on anything other than the practical went down before military science.

Murad Bey, the enemy commander, anchored his right flank on the village of Embabeh. Thoumas has General Rampon influential in the action here, implicitly in a position of principal command.

Though Rampon was certainly present at this battle, divisional commands were held on the day by Desaix, Reynier, Dugua, Vial and Bon. Louis Bon was killed later at Sainte Jean d'Acre and it is the case that at this point Rampon took over command of his division.

Bon's division certainly deployed into attack columns near the river and charged at the village of Embabeh. Antiquarian maps show forces under Rampon, detached from the Bon square, assaulting this village. The enemy garrison was routed and forced back against the river bank where its only possible means of escape was to swim across to the opposite side. Many infantry and Mamluk cavalry drowned in the attempt and we can deduce that it was in this part of the battlefield (based on the following reference) that Lasalle, on this occasion was active.

Whilst the wonderful battle paintings of Baron Louis-François Lejeune are rarely to be taken as snap-shots of action, but often rather composites which give the viewer a broad sense of the battle, his painting of the 'Battle of the Pyramids' is worthy of examination. At the far left, rear of the painting one can see the French of Rampon's command storming into a fortified village on the banks of the River Nile and the crushed, defeated garrison spilling out of the opposite side into the river as they attempt to flee.

★★★★★★

Antoine-Guillaume Rampon was a notable French Gen-

BATTLE OF

THE PYRAMIDS

eral of Division of the revolutionary period. He was active in the campaign in Italy being engaged in eight battles between 1796-7. In Egypt he fought a further seven battles including the Battle of Alexandria in 1801. In 1802 he took his place in the Senate and retired from the army.

★★★★★★

The following passage, which concerns Lasalle at, 'The Battle of the Pyramids' has been attributed by Thoumas to Rampon.

They (the Mamluks) wished to escape through Giseh (Giza), but Lasalle, with 60 hussars under his command, rushed upon them, drove them back into the camp, barred their way to Giseh, and forced them to throw themselves into the Nile to escape, where most of them were drowned. On the very evening of this battle, the success of which he had decided by his bold action, Lasalle was appointed *chef de brigade* by Bonaparte, and placed at the head of the 22nd Chasseurs à Cheval Regiment, one of the finest bodies of light cavalry corps, which fought in the course of our great wars.

Lasalle under the command of Desaix and at the head of the 22nd Chasseurs à Cheval on September 10th, according to Thoumas (August 11th, according to other sources), engaged the Mamluks again at Salahieh, a battle that remained famous for some time in the annals of the French Army because it was the first engagement in which the French cavalry found themselves in conflict with the Mamluks, without the benefit of the supporting aid of infantry.

Napoleon in his *Mémoirs* described the conflict:

On the 10th (September), at two o'clock in the afternoon, our cavalry consisting of 350 mounted soldiers arrived near the mosque of Salahieh; there they found Ibrahim Bey and his household ensconced. It was clear the enemy leader was well supported having with him 1,200 Mamluks and 500 Arabs under his command. The French infantry was still at two leagues distant from the enemy though two pieces of horse-artillery, and sixty mounted officers managed to join the cavalry to assist them. The heat was stifling in this season, at this time of the day and the infantry had the greatest difficulty in following along quickly upon the shifting sands.

However, our force soon engaged the cannonade; the French cavalry then made several charges and took two camels carrying two small pieces of cannon, and 150 other camels, loaded with not particularly valuable effects, which Ibrahim Bey abandoned to hasten the expedition of his escape.

Desperate not to allow this beautiful prize escape, Colonel Lasalle executed a new charge in which he lost about thirty men, killed or wounded, though without being able to force the enemy's rear-guard, which was composed of 600 Mamluks.

Monsieur le Marquis de Colbert, whose illustrious father Auguste Colbert, *aide-de-camp* of Murat, was appointed *chef d'escadron* on the evening of this affair, tells what follows, according to General Merlin, who was then himself Bonaparte's *aide-de-camp*:

> Two hundred men of the 7th Hussars and the 22nd Chasseurs rushed first and crossed blades with the Mamlukes, who fighting fiercely and with considerable skill, fell upon them. Their superior numbers soon surrounded our beleaguered cavalry and the entire *mêlée* disappeared within a cloud of dust, from which the firing of a few shots was heard, but it was chiefly the work of sword upon sword. The struggle was terrible but unequal. The Mamluks, mounted on supple and vigorous horses, wielded their arms with an unparalleled dexterity, often with deadly effect on the poor brave cavaliers, who were less well armed and mounted. The finely crafted sabres of the Mamlukes inflicted frightful wounds. The French cavalrymen sought to respond with sharp blows of their own, but all too often

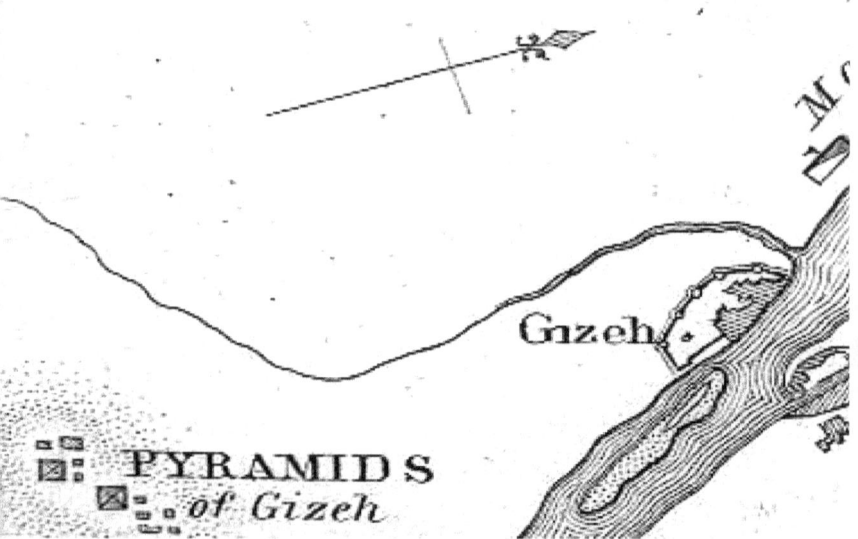

Map: Battle area near Cairo showing positions of Dugua, Menou, Regnier, Bon, Rampon, Desaix, Embabeh, Mourad Bey, Boulak, Ibrahim, Cairo, and Citadel along the Nile.

they were stopped making their mark on their opponents by the traditional thick clothes and coats of mail that the Mamluks habitually wore .... —Mis de Colbert, *Traditions et Souvenirs, tome 1er.*

Another perspective of this action can be found in Lasalle's service records which refer to the battle as follows:

> On September 10th, 1798, in the Salahieh battle Colonel Lasalle, having been disarmed in the combat, threw himself on the ground in the midst of the *mêlée*. He then picked up his fallen sabre, and, without abandoning his horse, fought on foot against the Mamluks who were all about him, wounding three of the enemy and also killing a horse. He eventually succeeded in remounting his own horse and rallied the hundred and eighty *chasseurs* and hussars under his command against the thousand or so Mamluks that remained to be fought.

Dragoon in Egypt, 1799

9. The Expedition to Upper Egypt, 1798–1799

Lasalle and his regiment (22nd Chasseurs à Cheval), which formed, with the 7th Hussars, the 15th and 21st Dragoons, Davout's cavalry command, played a significant role in the expedition of Upper Egypt under the orders of Desaix.

The heat was extreme, and the cavalry was incessantly engaged with the Mamluks, so this expedition was debilitating for the entire army. Lasalle was apparently highly regarded by the soldiers in the expedition for his good conduct and consideration under these trying circumstances. Regularly, when he came upon an infantryman, exhausted with fatigue and want, he allowed him to ride on one of his horses; sometimes he even dismounted to give him the one he rode himself. His personal positive attitude did not leave him in these most critical circumstances and this went some considerable way to support the morale of his troopers during the march.

On one occasion the water carried by the camels was exhausted, and so despite being in dire straits the column was forced of necessity to continue onwards to reach a place where they would find drinking water. A *chasseur* of the 22nd regiment, discovered a little brackish pool of the precious liquid and filled a goatskin with it which he deposited at the feet of his colonel. Lasalle, it was reported, shared it among the soldiers, without drinking any himself, although he was, of course, also virtually dying of thirst. It has been emphasised that whilst this displayed a great tenderness in Lasalle's personality as regarded his men, he also 'never found a soldier deaf to his voice when it came to marching or fighting.' Nevertheless, Lasalle's performance in the desert displayed the quality of leadership by example in its most easily understood form which also garnered affection, loyalty and confidence among the men under his command.

His service records indicate the actions in which he was particularly noted in Upper Egypt are those of Souaki, Redemeh, Thebes and Gehemmi.

★★★★★★★

The present author notes that, as is perfectly usual in older reference texts that the spelling of names of towns and villages especially in exotic locations, often vary. Similarly, a specific action may be referenced to one nearby location in a text but differently in another. Many authors have made it their mission to standardise these matters. However, having been through the process from both sides—writing and reading—this author's own view is that if the reader can understand the text's meaning this is not an especially important consideration. If two spellings are in regular use, then both are included for interest. Unfortunately, the same situation can apply to dates of events, numbers of men etc. It is quite apparent that original source material can be inconsistent on that subject so if that situation arises in this work the reader will be alerted to it.

★★★★★★

At Souaki, General Davout, returning from a reconnaissance with all his cavalry, which formed a total of 1,200 horses, met a gathering of 2,000 Arab cavalry and 5,000 infantry *fellahs*. An impetuous charge, which caused Lasalle to be cited in the general's report, put this enemy force into a headlong retreat which soon became a rout. The three regiments under Davout's command then took advantage of the chaos and made a horrible carnage among the *fellahs*.

At Redemeh (Rememieh), on January 18th, 1799 (according

to Thoumas), General Davout was engaged against very superior enemy forces. Some references place this engagement in 1798 quite soon after the Salahieh battle.

> Forced to fight alone in the heart of the engagement, the general was personally struggling in a combat against several Mamluks who were pressing him closely. Lasalle arrived with his regiment and threw himself into the *mêlée* and pushed his mount to the general's side. He seized a Mamluk who was preparing to strike Davout, and with a single blow from his sabre cut off his hands. He then, in the course of this action, broke his sabre on the head of Osman-Bey, the chief of the Mamlukes, broke his two pistols, commandeered the sword of a wounded dragoon, re-established the French initiative in the action, defeated the enemy force and chased the surviving enemy into the desert. (Extract from a report sent by the Minister of War to the Emperor on 8th June, 1804)

Whilst Thoumas makes no mention of it, Lassalle was also reported to have engaged in brilliant cavalry charges, which inflicted significant loss upon the enemy at Samanhout in late January, 1799.

Close by to Thebes (Luxor), on February 6th, 1799, Davout met Hassan-Bey, the principal lieutenant of Mourad, with his Mamluks. Hassan, seeing that he was principally dealing only with cavalry, had the 'audacity' (according to Thoumas) to come out to meet it head on. In probability this was less a matter of audacity and more the case that the Mamluks were well aware that in the cavalry charge and *mêlée* they were on equal terms with the French cavalry and, indeed, may have the advantage. In short, this was warfare as they understood it and they took their opportunity when they saw it for there was little to criticise the Mamluk cavalry in matters of courage. The shock of the engagement was terrible, but the 15th Dragoons, which formed the first French line, paused for a moment before the Mamluks to unload the contents of their firearms at them, and emptied the

Lasalle in combat in Egypt

saddles of those in the enemy first rank almost entirely by this fusillade.

The Mamlukes, however, rushed on with the charge, seeking to overwhelm the two wings of the French troops in order to surround them. The 22nd Chasseurs à Cheval, led by Lasalle, then moved at a fast trot to defeat this manoeuvre and the mêlée became general across the field.

Hassan Bey was dangerously wounded, after having had his horse killed under him. A *chef d'escadron* of the *chasseurs* regiment was killed with a sabre which cleft his skull in half. The Mamluks, satisfied at having bought time by fighting and so given the opportunity for their rich convoy to escape, at last abandoned the battlefield to the French.

Desaix in his report to General Bonaparte, on the expedition to Upper Egypt, says:

> The General, Davout, praises these two regiments (22nd Chasseurs and 7th Hussars), who received and furnished the charge with bravery and courage; he speaks with the greatest interest of the *chef de brigade* Lasalle, who, having killed a good number of his enemies, had his sabre broken to the hilt and who had the greatest good fortune of returning to safety without being hurt.

Lasalle was uncannily accustomed to this double circumstance: to have a broken sabre, and yet still able to retire without being wounded. According to his service record, he had seven sabres and a pair of broken pistols destroyed in the various actions in which he was engaged. He also had three horses killed, while no injuries to his person are shown on these same records. Understandably, this good fortune led him to believe to an extent in his own 'luck' or invulnerability. Indeed, the first blow that touched him was the one that killed him.

His close friend, Destrées (sometimes I think shown as Detres), who was with him as *chef d'escadron* in the 7th Hussars, and who was appointed colonel on the evening of the Salahieh battle, where he had been seriously wounded, was not so happy in this regard because he, by contrast, apparently received an injury almost in every battle in which he took part. Lasalle had another friend among the officers of the 7th Hussars during this period, Nicolas-Philibert Desvernois who wrote his military memoirs which provide corroborative information to that which we have concerning Lasalle. His own adventures in Egypt are also full of action typical of the light cavalry of his time and on one occasion he was rescued wounded from a dry canal in company with Jean Rapp who was at the time Bonaparte's *aide-de-camp*.

★★★★★★

Colonel Destrées was later appointed General and sent to the Army of Naples, where he remained until 1813, after which he was transferred to Germany at the head of a Neapolitan division of infantry and cavalry; This division was part of the garrison of Dantziek (Danzig: now Gdansk), during the long siege prosecuted against it. This defence, undertaken at a time of disaster for the French following the debacle of the Russian campaign, has received fewer laurels than it properly deserves particularly in respect of the excellent management of the capable commander of the besieged garrison, General Jean Rapp, his comrade from the Egyptian Campaign.

★★★★★★

Apparently, these two friends, (Lasalle and Destrées), as often happens with men possessed of fiery tempers, could neither live separately nor be united without quarrelling and fighting a duel. Destrées owed his life to Lasalle during the expedition to Upper Egypt, during which he had been dangerously wounded. The Arabs carried him almost dying through the desert, and Lasalle escorted the party to ensure his safety.

Lasalle walked away from his charge for a short time to seek water for the wounded in the party. The Arabs who had been left in charge of the wounded man, believed that he had permanently abandoned them and so were preparing to dispose of the apparently dying man by pre-emptively burying him when Lasalle returned just in time to prevent them from carrying out

MOUNTED MAMELUKE WARRIOR

this dark deed.

Possibly fearing his wrath, they immediately fled. Lasalle straight away pursued them and upon catching up to them prevented them from getting away and, with a great firmness of manner, ensured that they all returned to discharge the task that had been entrusted to them though he was, of course, significantly outnumbered by this Arab party. So essentially by a confident display determination Colonel Destrées was saved from what would have been an appalling death.

The most remarkable struggle Lasalle experienced in Upper Egypt was the engagement of Gehemmi, March 1st, 1799. Lasalle had been commanded to hold the post of Tahta. Suddenly he received word that a French officer was in imminent danger and urgently in need of rescue. Chef de Brigade Pinon (who was subsequently killed in Egypt) and his command was being threatened in nearby Siout by a gathering of rebellious Arabs. Without hesitation Lasalle gathered a force and rode to this officer's aid, effected the rescue and relieved Siout. However, during his absence, danger arose in his own post at Tahta, which was beset by a band of fanatics who had raised up all the surrounding countryside.

Immediately upon learning of this new threat, Lasalle retraced his steps and in his line of march unexpectedly discovered in the village of Gehemmi, a gathering of the fanatics. The report already quoted says:

> He surrounded this village with his regiment and marched with the infantry right into the face of the enemy, which resisted for several hours, and defended themselves with great determination in an enclosure which they had crenelated for the purpose. Realising they were bound to be defeated the enemy attempted to effect an escape, but during the break out they were furiously cut into pieces by the *chasseurs*. Left on the ground were more than 300 enemy corpses including that of their leader.'

When the small army of Desaix evacuated Upper Egypt, Lasalle

Lasalle in combat at Salahieh, 10 September, 1798

was placed, with a force composed of cavalry and infantry, at the camp of Belbeis. His mission was to secure the peace of the nearby countryside, the security of the road from Cairo to Suez for military traffic and the protection of the line of communications between Salahieh and Cairo.

It was from this final post in Egypt that Lasalle concluded his service in North Africa. Upon the receipt of the order he set out to return to France, after the convention of El Arich (El Arish) January 24th, 1800, at the same time as Generals Desaix and Davout. Lasalle came away from Egypt with an enhanced reputation and, following the style of the Mamluks, the voluminous trousers which became almost a trade-mark of his later colourful appearance.

These trousers, incidentally, were not necessarily, as may be imagined, merely an affectation of military fashion on Lasalle's part. Evidence that Lasalle was thinking, as usual about the efficiency of light cavalry work can be found concerning these trousers or overalls within the pages of de Brack's classic treatise, *Light Cavalry Outposts*.

In his book, when discussing clothing, de Brack writes:

> The best "trowsers" for campaign—those I would allow for officers—are those called, *"à la Lasalle'*. They are wide with pockets and the false leather boots with which they are provided serve the purpose of ensuring they are not worn out too soon. Also, they are not spoiled by mud for they can be wiped clean and dry with a sponge in a moment.

He concludes his verdict on clothing as follows:

> Anything that simplifies the dress of a light cavalryman, and shortens the time he takes in dressing, thus fulfilling the first conditions of getting under arms, seems to me to be preferable.

So, these are essentially 'campaign trousers' and thus it would probably be quite wrong to assume they were permanent fixture of Lasalle's appearance at any time. There seems little doubt that Lasalle can be properly credited with the innovation of this style of cavalry overall. Of course, other people are wont to copy good ideas whether for reasons of fashion or practicality. In the modern era, indeed, a trouser style created for farm work has become an unassailable fashion icon. Conversely, and perhaps not unexpectedly, military dandies took the theme of the wide cavalry trouser as fashion to extremes.

During the first part of the campaign to Russia, there is an eye witness report of a fashion conscious French *aide-de-camp*, upon being sent on foot on an urgent errand, falling to the ground in a heap, his extra wide trousers having become tangled in his spurs. In fury, embarrassment and exasperation, the young man took out his sword and cut away the legs of the garment at the knees and then raced away to all purposes appearing to be wearing 'shorts'.

The 'Lasalle', trousers in confirmation of their practical legitimacy, endured in the French light and heavy cavalry into the 20th century becoming an established part of campaign uniform.

7th Hussars in Egypt

10. The Captured Lasalle Letters from Egypt

We are fortunate that two letters exist written by Lasalle from the time he was serving in Egypt. 'The Battle of the Nile' naval conflict dealt a crippling blow to the French fleet in the Mediterranean. Thereafter, it was still possible for French ships to navigate between France and Egypt, but the journey was a perilous one and many vessels were intercepted by the Royal Navy to be either sunk or taken as prizes. These French ships were, of course, employed in carrying documents, both official and personal, to France and these letters were avidly read by the British, as correspondence has always been, ever since the notion of military intelligence gathering was conceived.

On one of these occasions the captured ship was carrying two personal letters from Lasalle. The letters appeared in a book accompanied by comments (published in Dublin in 1799 and translated into English) among other letters written by French soldiers in Egypt of the *Armée d'Orient* which had been intercepted at sea by the fleet under Nelson.

One letter is addressed to Lasalle's mistress (eventually to become his wife) and other to his mother. It is not suggested that one can discern much of the complete man from two letters, especially when they are both written to women and each of those held a position of affection and intimacy, in their own ways, within Lasalle's life. Nevertheless, this is the appropriate place to include them since they pertain to Lasalle's time in Egypt and since, undeniably, the reader may hear the voice of the subject of this book albeit confined to its most tender and considerate tones.

Grand Cairo, August 7th.

C. Lasalle, Chief of Brigade of the 22nd Regiment of Chasseurs à Cheval, of the Army of the East, to his Mother.

On the eve of setting out with the commander in chief, to intercept a most valuable caravan, which the Mamelukes have seized, and which must, at all events, be wrested out of their hands, I learn, my dear mother, that a courier is preparing to leave Cairo. Opportunities occur so seldom, that I cannot think of letting this escape without giving you a line.

Neither fatigue, nor heat, nor the privation of wine, have hitherto had the smallest effect on my health; on the contrary, I get flesh every day. I have but one thing to regret, and that is my poor hair, which is all fallen off through the excessive heat; assisted, I believe, in some degree, by my total want of powder and pomatum.

General Bonaparte, always prodigal of his kindness, has given me the command of the mounted troops of the 7th Hussars, and the 22nd Chasseurs. Here I am then, a little General! he often invites me to dinner, and always places me at his right hand. I have an infinite deal of trouble to form my new corps, which is in the most ruinous state you can possibly conceive—by dint of incessant exertions, however, I hope to succeed to my honour.

We are assured that in the course of a few months, reinforcements from France will arrive here, and that we shall then return home. This is the wish of the whole army, which, though as well circumstanced as it is possible to be in a country like this, is too truly French in heart, not to prefer its native land to Egypt!

We have already 800 Arabian horses, excellent runners—I have three for my own share. The officers of my regiment behave extremely well and have given me many striking proofs of their esteem.

Happily, in consequence of my new employ, I have little time for reflection, and am too much fatigued when night comes, to dream wide awake—Without this, I feel that I should sink under the wretchedness I experience, from the consideration that I am far removed from everything that is dear to me in the world—from my mother, my father, my mistress, and my little boy. Sometimes, however, sad ideas, bitter regrets will force themselves upon me; a sigh breaks forth, trickles down my cheek, and I hasten to tear myself from my melancholy reverie—O poor Charles! how art thou passing thy youth! O duty! why art thou so rigorous!

I flatter myself that the same kind providence which has hitherto accompanied me in the heat of battle, has also watched over your life. I anticipate the pleasure I shall one day have in kissing your honoured hand, and in drying up, by my embraces, the tears you have not ceased to shed for me.—O my dearest mother! I want—I cannot express how much I want, to fold you in my arms!

My faithful Joseph is still with me. He is extremely useful, and I cannot tell you how much I am indebted to his care and attention, I have no doubt but that you are just as much indebted to Colin for his, and I therefore seriously promise him a fine Indian shawl, &c. if we seize the caravan.

Adieu,—take a thousand tender kisses, and present my respectful duty to my aged father, whom I love and revere.

My kind remembrances to all my friends, and respects where they are due,

Charles Lasalle.

When these letters were first published by the British for a British readership it should be remembered that the war with France was still being fought. All the letters in the book in which they appeared were accompanied by editor's footnotes addressed to a British public ostensibly to illuminate and expand upon

Mamelukes and a Bedoween Arab

the captured documents. All of these footnotes are predictably couched in the most partisan form and many of them for this reason are not worth republishing, especially as they often bore entirely on the conduct of personalities rather than the courses of history. Bearing in mind the above, one example follows, since it not only provides an insight to the times from perspective of the enemy but concerns in greater detail the subject of the caravan attack mentioned in Lasalle's letter.

> It will afford no small satisfaction, we believe, to most of our readers, to know that this valuable caravan escaped the hands of this rapacious *banditti* (The French in this case). They came up with it, indeed, as we learn from several of the letters, but found it covered in so masterly a manner by Ibrahim Bey, and so gallantly defended by his handful of Mamelukes, that the French, after several ineffectual attempts, and losing the greatest part of their new-raised cavalry (alas! For poor Charles!) were compelled to make a disgraceful retreat before less than half their numbers!
> It appears (and we mention it for the exclusive benefit of the admirers of the "invincible Bonaparte," who commanded in person) that the Mamelukes not only fought with more bravery, but with more skill than their opponents; and that if Ibrahim had not judged, and rightly judged, it more expedient to secure his convoy, than to pursue his baffled enemy, very few of them would have got back to Cairo, to amuse the world with a splendid narrative of their triumphant expedition towards Syria!
> In the contest we have mentioned, there were no cannon on either side. This even furnished a most important lesson, which we trust the Mamelukes will never forget. They will not in future encumber themselves with an artillery which they cannot serve, nor attack their enemies when protected by it. They will content themselves with harassing them, with failing on detached parties unprovided with those formidable means of offence; and their superior courage and activity will eventually reduce the

French to the necessity of surrendering at discretion.

The present writer wishes to draw the reader to the reference in the sixth paragraph of Lasalle's letter to 'my mistress, my little boy' in the light of what follows. The second letter is addressed, indeed, to Lasalle's mistress, Joséphine who was at this time still married to General Berthier.

Grand Cairo (*20 Thermidor*), August 7th.
C. Lasalle, Chief of Brigade, &c. &c. to his Joséphine.

I have not yet heard from you, my much-regretted Joséphine. Somehow or other, the three couriers which had reached Malta in safety, were unfortunately dispatched from thence in the same vessel,—this was taken by the English, and all the letters were thrown into the sea. It has swallowed worlds of wealth; but never yet a treasure that equalled, in my esteem, a single letter of yours!

I am on the eve of setting off with the 7th Hussars, and my own regiment. General Bonaparte, who overwhelms me with kindness and attention, has just given me the command of them. We are going to meet a caravan which the Mamelukes have seized, and which is very valuable. We shall certainly have a struggle for it; but good fortune, and you, who have hitherto protected me, will assuredly preserve me once more.

You ought to have received three of my letters from Malta, and one from Alexandria: this is now the second from Cairo. I cannot write to you oftener. I am absolutely worn out with constant exertions to organise my new corps, which is in a most wretched state.

Your brother regards me with kindness, because you are not here: would it were the reverse! How is my bantling? What a sweet little fellow he will be when I see him again?—Yes, I shall soon return—General Bonaparte has promised that fresh troops shall speedily arrive from France to relieve us. But then how ugly shall I be! The heat has turned us all as black as crows; and, to complete my misfortunes, I have lost all my hair.

How do you proceed in your pregnancy?—Good heavens! how distressing it is to live in a state of constant uncertainty respecting all that is dear to me!

The days of happiness are passed. If I cease to exert myself but for a moment, my mind becomes a prey to the most gloomy reflections. I weep, and no one partakes my grief. I have not a single acquaintance in the regiment, nor a friend in the country. Poor Charles! thou hast lost everything in losing thy Joséphine. Do you at least regret me, and I shall not be wholly miserable. I may forget that I have been happy beyond the lot of human nature,—but to forget that you are my best beloved, or to think of living without you, is what can never enter into my mind.

Adieu:—my horse is at the door, I send you a thousand kisses.

Your own Charles

Since correspondence to Lasalle's mistress has been included at this point it is appropriate to make further reference to their relationship. Joséphine Jeanne Marguerite d'Aiguillon was married to Victor Leopold Berthier who was the younger brother of Louis-Alexander Berthier, eventually to become a Marshal of France.

Victor, in fact married his sister-in-law and the marriage produced three sons, Almeric (born 1797), Oscar (born 1798) and Alexandre (born 1800). By 1799 he was General of Division and also served in Egypt. The circumstances of Joséphine's affair with Lasalle are not known in detail, other than to note it embraced personages of far greater influence than Lasalle (which made it more than usually, potentially perilous) and that it had been carried on for some time before it caused the Berthier's to divorce in 1802. The rigours of campaigning eventually wore out Leopold physically and he resigned from the army, dying in Paris in 1807.

Lasalle married Joséphine Berthier and the marriage brought forth one child, a daughter, Joséphine Charlotte. After Leopold

Berthier's death, Lasalle adopted the three Berthier children and raised them as his own, to the point of naming them as his heirs.

Readers of Lasalle's letter to Joséphine will note that Lasalle affectionately refers within it to '*his* bantling' (small boy) which must refer to Oscar and is solicitous on the subject of Joséphine's pregnancy which refers to the child who would be, upon his birth, Alexandre. Added to this, we have the reference to '*my little boy*' in the letter to Lasalle's mother.

Whilst none of the foregoing is other than circumstantial from the perspective of evidence, this correspondence prompts us to speculate that Lasalle had reason to believe that he was possibly the natural father of one and possibly both of these children. It is also tempting to imagine there was a connection with Alexandria, given it was topical at the time, in the naming of the child, Alexandre though this offers no illumination as to the actual father since both paternal candidates served in Egypt. Lasalle makes no particular reference to Almeric in his enquiries or in this concerned context—presumably, since he was unambiguously Leopold's legitimate son.

All the children subsequently bore the combined surnames of both Berthier and Lasalle becoming known as Berthier de Lasalle. The seniority of Almeric was not subordinated following this change in the status of the children suggesting that no distinction was made between them irrespective of their paternity. Almeric became Comte Berthier de Lasalle and Oscar and Alexandre both became Baron Berthier de Lasalle. Joséphine Lasalle died in 1850 aged 78 years.

11. The Expedition to Spain & Portugal, 1799-1803

The War of the Second Coalition began with some inevitability in 1798 though very little of great moment occurred until 1799 when the allies mounted several invasions bringing about campaigns in Switzerland, Italy and the Netherlands, which introduced a new nation to the battlefield within an Anglo-Russian alliance. The allies did well initially, suffered reverses and squabbles, which motivated the Russians to withdraw from the coalition. Meanwhile, Bonaparte had returned from Egypt to France, mounted a *coup* which made him First Consul and with the title effectively placed himself at the head of the French Government. The Napoleonic era was about to begin.

Napoleon sent Moreau off to campaign in Germany. He then raised a new army and marched through Switzerland so he could attack the Austrians in the rear via northern Italy, met them in battle at Marengo, June 14th, 1800, and won a narrow victory. The French then occupied northern Italy. Moreau had invaded Bavaria and beat the Austrians resoundingly at Hohenlinden, in early December, 1800 marching on Vienna and inspiring the Austrians to sue for peace.

★★★★★★

Hohenlinden was Moreau's last victory for France. He was opposed to Napoleon's aggrandisement, arrested and forced into exile. He was killed at the Battle of Dresden in 1813 whilst in conversation with the *Tsar* by a shot from his own countrymen.

COLONEL OF HUSSARS

✶✶✶✶✶✶

Lasalle did not take part in the campaign of Marengo (14th June, 1800) which cost the life of one of his former commanders, General Desaix, but on the 25th June, 1800 he was appointed Colonel of the 10th Hussars and attached, with his new regiment, to the reserve cavalry of the Italian Army commanded by Davout.

On the 17th of January, 1801, apparently, and therefore a few days after the signing of The Armistice of Steyer (25th December 1800) which terminated the revolutionary wars, he distinguished himself once again at Civitella, where, at the head of a single squadron, he charged and defeated six 'enemy' squadrons. (Report of the Minister of War to the Emperor, dated June 8th, 1804)

Among the colonels of the light cavalry, Lasalle was by this point probably the most renowned. Since the campaign of 1796 he had continually provided his superiors with proofs of his courage and command abilities on the field of war. The Lasalle of peacetime was an entirely different proposition and during the four years of peace which followed the campaign of 1801 and the Treaty of Lunéville, Lasalle's propensities found few ways to express themselves other than in the indulgence of his pleasures.

Lasalle's regiment was one among the troops sent from Italy to the south of France in 1801 becoming part of the Corps of Observation of the Gironde. Of this period General Foy wrote:

> French troops (of this corps) in 1801 crossed the Pyrenees, traversed Spain and imposed a burthensome capitulation on Portugal.

This brief war, known as 'The War of the Oranges' was principally fought by the Spanish though certainly at the instigation of the French and with the intention of their active military support.

Lasalle and his men were to be part of the army which was intended to be sent to fight in Portugal under the orders of

Gouvion Saint-Cyr, who was soon to be replaced by General Charles-Victor Leclerc. This army crossed the Pyrenees to join the campaign with Spanish troops, and the Lasalle's regiment occupied quarters in Salamanca.

The soldiers of the 10th Hussars were well disciplined and, of course, very handsome in their powder blue uniforms with red facings. At this time, they came not as invaders, but as allies of the Spanish Government and so they were everywhere well received in the country, and the chronicle assures us that the Colonel of the 10th Hussars found the Spanish ladies were quite as impressed with him as were the beautiful Italian women who had been besotted in 1796 with Captain Lasalle. This was hardly surprising since he was still only twenty-six years old, handsome, confident and wore the most glittering hussar uniform to perfection.

His self-assuredness invariably crossed the line into arrogance. It is reported that on one occasion he came to the home of a highly regarded lady of Salamanca, accompanied by the refrains of his regimental musicians, and at noon gave her a serenade. General Victor, commanding one of the infantry divisions of the army, happened to be lodged with this lady, and asked Lasalle what was happening.

'Oh, it is not for you, General,' replied the colonel with aplomb, 'but a serenade for *Madame*.'

The lady, who was present, protested at this decidedly unorthodox timing for a serenade which as most know is traditionally sung in the moonlight under a lady's window.

'But, sir,' she exclaimed,' it is yet full daylight!'

'That is another good reason why I am here now, *Madame*,' replied Lasalle, meaning, of course, so the lady could fully appreciate him in all his military magnificence.

The army of General Leclerc passed across Spain and almost reached its destination but, in the event, did not advance beyond the fortified town of Almeida on the Spanish and Portuguese border, where it was halted by the news of the peace treaty (The Treaty of Badajoz, June 6th, 1801) concluded between Spain and Portugal. All the troops destined for this operation would in due course return to France unblooded including the 10th Hussars and their colonel who, to his disappointment, had been deprived of the action that gave him focus and purpose.

Young officers, accustomed to the latitudes afforded to them whilst living for six years in conquered countries, found it difficult to accommodate themselves within the tedium and strictures of garrison life. It was during this period of Lasalle's life in Spain that originated the many follies which, with more or less accuracy, have been attributed to Lasalle. His reputation for perpetual boisterous behaviour was perhaps slightly exaggerated, but it was as at least as well-deserved as one may expect of a young cavalier who had enjoyed complete liberty since the campaign in Italy. As a poet has said very well:

When on a Lasalle one wants to model oneself
It is by the beautiful sides that he must resemble

General de Brack, who had served under Lasalle's orders in this famous brigade of hussars in 1806 noted somewhat more directly and caustically:

Nature, by pleasing herself to perfect, to complete this unique example (Lasalle as a soldier), had largely endowed it in three ways: with moral, intellectual and physical strength. The stamp of good taste and distinction was imprinted on all his actions. The so-called Lasalle of peace is nothing but a shameful Falstaff and inspires nothing but pity and disgust.

General de Brack was apparently addressing officers here, who were working to be comparable to Lasalle in the ranks of the light cavalry in an attempt to advise balance and some moderation of behaviour. That young officers would attempt to become soldiers in wartime in the Lasalle model, was eminently desirable. That they should believe this paragon of military character must inevitably combine with the behaviour of a rake in peacetime was less so. In short, in its entirety, there was only room for one version of Antoine Charles Louis de Lasalle in the army of France and that was the original one. One cannot ignore any of the features of Lasalle's character—the admirable or the reprehensible to appreciate the total man.

★★★★★★

Antoine de Brack was a well-known and well regarded light cavalry officer who served with the famous 2nd Regiment of Lancers of the Imperial Guard—'The Red Lancers' from 1812-15. Today he is most well-known for his instructional book, *Cavalry Outpost Duties*.

★★★★★★

According to General Thiébault, Lasalle and his friends had, during their stay in Spain, in 1801, formed an elite society known as the '*Altérés*'. The name is perhaps telling since it suggests that Lasalle's status ran so high that others were quite prepared to be identified as a group having conduct which 'emulated' his own examples.

Essentially this was a personality cult where the object of adoration of the membership was always present to dictate behaviour by example. It is demonstrative that he did not intend these to be 'good examples' by the terms that most people would understand, since it was forbidden for the members, under an agreed penalty imposed for transgressions, not to be thirsty. In short, every member of this society was obliged to be perpetually intoxicated and what this group then embarked upon would be whatever came about as a consequence of this edict.

There are references to a club formed under Lasalles influence under the name of, 'The Society of Alcoholics' and also in an English translation of Thiébault's recollections, 'The Thirsty Souls'. We can assume that all these were titles given at the time or later for the same society. Given the accuracy and meaning of the French name '*Altérés*', the present writer would suggest, 'The Copycats' as an appropriate modern colloquial title.

That said, there can be no doubt that the imbibing of as much alcohol as possible was a core principle of this society and its members set about their responsibilities to it with enthusiasm and commitment. Thiébault noted:

> I forget how many lunatics belonged to it (the Society), but what is certain is that in less than a month they had drunk all the foreign wine in Salamanca. Once, when he (Lasalle) had been giving me a score of empty bottles, I said, "Do you want to kill yourself?"
>
> "My dear friend", he replied, "a hussar who is not dead by the time he is thirty is a dirty scoundrel. I am making my arrangements not to pass that limit."

The present writer has noted any number of derisive titles appended to this quotation but is of the opinion that most of them amount to the same meaning with the exception of the word, 'coward'. Lasalle had every reason to expect his officers to be brave and in this case, to give him his due, he is referring to what he considered (by no means uniquely) to be essential to the guiding spirit of the character of a light cavalry officer.

This quotation, attributed to Lasalle is one of the most well-known concerning him and its context is worth noting because whilst Lasalle clearly did not exclude reckless bravery (or make the point to include it for that matter) as the cause of legitimate early demise of a light cavalryman, he likewise did not exclude the same outcome as a result of what more sober judges might consider to be mere dissolution. Given his examples, we can only deduce that, despite his reputation as a prankster on this subject he was not joking.

Thiébault commented:

> Lassalle contrived to put infinite grace into things of the least graceful kind. I mean that with his charming manners he was a drinker, a libertine, a gambler and a rowdy practical joker.

Another anecdote from Thiébault concerning Lasalle's time in Salamanca is worthy of inclusion not least because many of us have, bar the details, seen the comic circumstances of it in motion pictures. A certain captain of engineers apparently had an attractive mistress who soon became the focus of Lasalle's roving eye despite his 'writing a tender letter every day to his own wife'. Lasalle's interest in the lady evolved to action, which in turn provoked a challenge from the aggrieved captain. The duel was proposed to be with sabres, a weapon with which 'Lasalle, both strong and lissom, was the most dangerous man in existence'.

The opinion of all who knew of the approaching combat was that unless Lasalle intended to be uncharacteristically and fatally generous to his opponent on this occasion the captain of engineers was a doomed man. It was also certain that Lasalle, who his own friends felt able to term 'a demon', would play with his prey for his own amusement and the fun of the spectacle as a cat would with a mouse.

Lasalle knew very well that he had a huge advantage over his opponent and so from the outset of the duel abstained altogether from attacking and confined himself to parrying, but did so with such force against the incoming sabre blows that the captain's wrist began to lose its strength. The duel, without resolution, went on until the captain had to call a temporary halt to rest at which point Lasalle, 'would skip around him amid a thousand jokes, monkey tricks and grimaces, giving him a spank on the bottom with the flat of his sabre then dance off in bursts of laughter'.

Lasalle relentlessly repeated this performance 'ten times' by which time the captain, though frustrated and furious, was utterly exhausted. When it was clear his opponent could stand no more of this kind of treatment Lasalle put an end to the contest reportedly saying:

> If you had known me better you would have attached less importance to the incident that has vexed you. Had I known you better I should have abstained from poaching on your preserves. Accept this declaration and let us end this unequal contest which has only served to show still plainer what a man of honour you are.

This quotation apparently shows Lasalle to be, in the final analysis, a good and generous fellow though it should be recognised he might just as easily disarmed his opponent on several occasions within the first minutes of the duel without putting him through an extended period of physical debilitation and personal humiliation, which was tantamount to torture. Having done so, however, given his fame, wounding or dispatching the captain (a subordinate officer) would have required some problematic explanations to any authority investigating the matter. So, in concluding the affair Lasalle displayed as much prudence as magnanimity, all be it unilateral.

Equally, from the captain's perspective, acceptance of Lasalle's verdict would be something of a *fait accompli* regardless of how he genuinely felt about the matter, given the already demonstrated certain alternatives.

At this point the sincerity of Lasalle's words are at best open to question. One may be minded of Lady Caroline Lamb's comment regarding Lord Byron that he was 'mad, bad and dangerous to know'. Lasalle appears to be capable of practically anything dependent upon how the mood took him at the time.

Apparently, on one occasion in Salamanca, Lasalle had spent a night on the town with one of his officers, and they were returning together to bed the following morning. Suddenly the colonel assumed a serious air, and looking at his companion:

'Sir,' he said, 'you have just passed a night in a debauchery that is frightful! Go to prison.' 'And he went,' added General Thiébault. (*Souvenirs de Roederer* already quoted.)

Another anecdote from Thiébault has left us a telling insight to Lasalle's character. It was well known that whilst in Salamanca he practised music for three hours each day and often played with Thiébault since both were keen musicians. All the French officers had time on their hands and many became bored with their routine existence in Spain. Lassalle, according to Thiébault, kept them 'alive with all kinds of occupations and by his incomparable fun'.

At dinner one evening, Lasalle announced that, 'I have given the general a taste for shooting, restored Thiébault's taste for music and awakened in General Monnet a taste for intelligence!'

★★★★★★

It seems that Lasalle was as reckless with his tongue as he was in his actions and there is no doubt that there is something compelling about a person that goes his own way in every respect, heedless and presumably indifferent to the consequences. Most soldiers know it is inadvisable to make this kind of remark about a superior officer when it is certain that the insult will eventually come to his ears. Peculiarly, Louis Claude Monnet de Lorbeau did have a chequered military career, but at the time Lasalle was making him butt of his humour, there had been little left to us in the history of his former career to that point, which would indicate he was other than a competent and brave senior officer. Perhaps Lasalle could see something in Monnet that histories do not record.

Nevertheless, in 1803, concerning Monnet's performance in the Low Countries, Napoleon is on record of expressing his complete confidence in him. However, neither General Monnet's good standing with the emperor nor his good fortune in his military career were fated to long endure. In 1809 he was given command, for the second time, of Vlissingen and Walcheren, and not only bungled the disposition of the defensive positions of area but met the enemy force of approaching 20,000 British troops with such a small proportion of the resources at his disposal that he failed to prevent them from landing from their transports. Vlissingen was surrendered and, on this occasion, Napoleon was disinclined to be lenient with the architect of the defeat.

Monnet was tried *in absentia*, convicted of cowardice and treason and sentenced to death. Returning to France and respectability with the Bourbon Restoration in 1814, Monnet was reinstated as a general officer in the Royalist Army but removed again from the list of general officers in Napoleon's brief reign during 'The Hundred Days'. Of course, Monnet's status changed yet again after the fall of Napoleon, but he was unable to gain much profit from his position because four years later he died in Paris in 1819, just 53 years old.

12. Lasalle in Peacetime, 1803-1805

With no war to fight and no legitimate reason, for the time being, to remain in Spain Lasalle returned to France. Several anecdotes concerning him from this period may come from the journey from Iberia towards his destination in 1804 to the camp of Boulogne, that is to say in the vicinity of Saint-Omer and Calais.

According to an unverified account by one of his biographers, (Bégin, *Biographie de la Moselle*), Lasalle, who was in garrison at Niort in western France 'at the beginning of the Empire', would have gone one evening to a show after having dined well, and seeing on stage, several soldiers of his regiment among the extras, he would have suddenly exclaimed: *"À moi, hussards!"*

Whereupon the extras would have left the stage to run, dressed in Romans or Greeks, with their colonel, and the performance would have remained unfinished. Although this anecdote has the appearance of Lassalle's brand of humour it lacks the authenticity of confirmation because the 10th Hussars, at the beginning of the Empire, was not garrisoned at Niort; it was stationed in 1803 and at the beginning of 1804 at Agen.

The regiment in garrison at Niort at that time was the 22nd Chasseurs à Cheval, of which Lasalle had been the colonel and adored by all during the campaign of Egypt, and which Colonel La Tour-Maubourg, his friend, commanded in 1804-1805. So, the story has the potential to be true especially since Lasalle was obviously capable of this kind of mischief. The ringing tones of their former commanding officer would have most soldiers running to his side irrespective of whether he called them hussars or *chasseurs*. La Tour-Maubourg was a kindred spirit, unlikely to protest at such antics.

★★★★★★

Victor de Fay de la Tour-Maubourg served all though the Napoleonic Wars until the Battle of Leipzig when a small calibre ball seriously wounded his leg. It is perhaps a measure of the man that upon noticing that his servant was weeping in distress at the severity of his wound, La Tour-Maubourg exclaimed, 'What are you crying for, you idiot? Now you have one less boot to clean!' Fortunately, for La Tour-Maubourg, the celebrated French military surgeon, Baron Larrey was at hand and he reported that 'he effected an amputation below the thigh under enemy fire in less than three minutes'. La Tour-Maubourg did not rally to Napoleon during 'The Hundred Days' having sworn allegiance to the Bourbons. He notably sat on the tribunal which sentenced Marshal Ney to death.

★★★★★★

It is possible that Lasalle, travelling from Agen to Boulogne with the 10th Hussars, made a detour to visit the 22nd Chasseurs à Cheval who he had not seen since his departure from Egypt. He arrived at Niort, which would certainly be very little distance out of his way, dined with his former officers and went thereafter to the theatre with them.

The problem for the biographer is that there are so many anecdotes of Lassalle's outrageous behaviour and sparkling repartee that it is hard (probably impossible) to know which ones to believe because they are all founded on hearsay. This is a shame since most are entertaining and all reveal a lively prankster indulging himself to the full.

One attribution in particular that is worthy of investigation is the assertion that Lasalle, on the eve of the Battle of Marengo, at Napoleon's table no less, composed the famous French drinking song '*Fanchon*' which is still sung to this day. According to Thoumas, Lasalle was not present at Marengo, but in any event,

A HUSSAR ENJOYING HIS WINE AND TOBACCO

'*Fanchon*', a song based on a real female street singer, had been in the French military drinking song repertoire for some time before Lasalle ever lifted a glass of wine to his lips. It is reliably claimed that '*Fanchon*' was written around 1757 by the cleric, Abbé Gabriel-Charles de Lattaignant. In 1800 the Theatre of Vaudeville actually created a record concerning '*Fanchon*' by playing the song 400 times in a row. It is, given his appetites, almost a certainty that Lasalle sang '*Fanchon*' lustily and more than once, but that is some distance from his being the composer of the song.

Another biographer tells us that Lasalle struck the person of the *prefect* of Niort with a whip in the middle of a ball. There is fact at the foundation of this assertion in the broader sense. The *prefect* of Agen, giving a great official ball, had invited neither the colonel nor the officers of the 10th Hussars to attend. Lasalle, however, took this omission as a slight and went to the event with all his officers to protest against the implied insult to the regiment. There then followed what has been described as 'a most lively scene', after which Lasalle sent for a picket of hussars whom he had instructed to be ready, and upon his order these *hussars*, entering into the ballroom, threw the supper, which had been prepared for the legitimate guests out through the windows.

The next day the *prefect* went to Paris to complain about this behaviour, and Lasalle did the same to put his side of the story. The affair was brought in front of Napoleon for consideration. The great man's verdict was perhaps dependably pragmatic in his own interests.

'All that is required is a signature to make a *prefect*,' said Napoleon on this occasion, 'a Lasalle cannot be made in twenty years.'

The colonel was arrested for thirty days; a virtual rap on the knuckles, whereas the *prefect* was dismissed from his office. The rationale was typical of Napoleon in that, according to his philosophy, one must expect a hussar to behave as a hussar and anyone who treated one differently in the belief that he would not, for whatever reason, behave true to type must be stupid and so unworthy an office that required sound judgement as a prerequisite. A long report addressed to Napoleon by the Minister of War, on behalf of Colonel Lasalle, on June 8th, 1804, seems to have been written at that period

The destination of the 10th regiment of Hussars was the great camp at Boulogne on the English Channel (La Manche) coast of France was created by Napoleon in 1803 as a mustering point for the army preparatory to the planned invasion of Britain. It existed until 1805 but, of course, never saw the fulfilment of its purpose since the Royal Navy dominated the seaways and a successful crossing in the face of superior opposition was destined for disaster. Between 60,000 and 200,000 French troops were based at Boulogne at one time or another. At its most fully occupied it contained the proposed invasion force of the so called, 'Army of Ocean Coasts' or 'Army of England'.

Napoleon reputedly proclaimed, 'Let us be masters of the Channel for six hours and we shall be masters of the world.' However, the British naval blockade held firm and he called off the invasion, breaking up the camp from late August 1805 and marching the army eastwards to fight the Ulm and Austerlitz campaign.

However, the Boulogne camp saw the distribution by Napoleon's own hand of some of the early awards of the Legion of Honour medal in August, 1804. Lasalle had already been awarded the *Légion d'Honneur* at the time of the institution of the order, in September 24th, 1803, and a Commander of the Legion of Honour, in June 14th, 1804 according to Thoumas.

The first appointment was his by right, Lasalle having been awarded a sabre and a pair of pistols 'of honour' on the 5th of August, 1800, but the second appointment was a most flattering distinction, because in the great promotion of the 14th of June, 1804, among officers, three cavalry colonels only, received *La Croix de Commandant*: Marulaz, Lasalle, and his friend and comrade of Egypt, Destrées. Only one colonel of infantry, incidentally, was the object of the same favour.

★★★★★★

LASALLE, GÉNÉRAL DE BRIGADE

en uniforme de dragon

(1805)

We have touched already upon the career of Destrées so no further comment is required here. Jacob François Marulaz was born in Zeiskam (now in Germany) and joined the Esterházy Hussars of the French Royalist Army in 1784 as a trooper. He fought with distinction throughout the revolutionary wars and under Napoleon during the empire period rising to the rank of General of Division. Notably this hussar, who was wounded 19 times in action and had 26 horses killed under him, was close to Lasalle at the Battle of Wagram when the fatal bullet struck him. Seeing that the troopers of the 8th Hussars were shaken by the death of Lasalle he reminded them that he was once their colonel and concluded, 'You will charge. Marulaz is at your head.' Marulaz was then shot in the arm but would not relinquish command until a cannon ball killed his horse and he was stunned in the resulting fall. He joined Napoleon during 'The Hundred Days', so was forced by the Bourbon Restoration to retire from the army in 1815.

★★★★★★

The many acts of bravery and boldness executed by Lasalle, were well known to the Emperor Napoleon, since several of them had been accomplished before the eyes of General Bonaparte. So predictably relieved of the Emperor's anger (The First Consul was now Emperor Napoleon crowned by his own hand at the Louvre in Paris, December 2nd, 1804) concerning his wild behaviour when there were no enemies of France to fight, Lasalle was appointed brigadier general on February 1st, 1805 (21 *pluviose an XIII*). No doubt the emperor well knew there would be need for Lasalle's practical talents soon enough.

This grand promotion included, among the *divisionnaires*, Mathieu Dumas, Caffarelli, Broussier, Léopold Berthier, Lauriston, Caulaincourt, Savary, Espagne, Mermet, among the brigadiers together with General Lasalle: Mouton (the future Maréchal of Lobau), Defrance, Eugène Merlin, Marulaz, Ruffin, Taviel and Pernety.

Thanks to a divorce, the two husbands of the same woman could be seen on this promotion list. On December 5th, 1803, Lasalle had married Joséphine-Jeanne-Marguerite d'Aiguillon, the divorced wife of General Léopold Berthier, the brother of the major-general, and it is said withal, 'a charming woman, apparently, endowed with all the graces'. One of them was not fidelity to her first husband as has been described.

However, this marriage proved to be the genuine love of both Lasalle and his wife, for Madame Lasalle followed her husband in some of his campaigns, and even attended several battles, the last of which was that of Medina de Rio Seco against regular and militia Spanish forces during the Peninsular War, July 14th, 1808. Cannon and musket balls were falling all around her and her little girl on that day and she was seized with terror. Lasalle instructed her to quit the battlefield where upon she then retired to a nearby ambulance and 'performed the office of lady of charity' in assisting with the care of the wounded. Lasalle was an excellent husband (presumably by the standards of the day) whose love for his wife was as committed as his conviction for everything he undertook. The last sentence of the last letter he wrote to his wife has often been cited:

> My heart is for you, my blood to the emperor and my life to honour.

Since we are on the subject of anecdotes, we must relate that of Napoleon, who is reported to have offered Lasalle an appointment to be his First Squire, to which proposal Lasalle is said to have replied:

> You can make me general because I am fighting for France, but I do not want to be your domestic. (Bégin, *Biographie de la Moselle*).

Once again this is a story that is hard to verify especially since it lacks a fair amount of plausibility. It would seem unlikely that Napoleon wished to attach to his household a man whose independent character did not suit any of the requirements of the job title. To put the issue more bluntly, Lasalle was certain to be a great deal of trouble in any situation when he did not have a war to fight and Napoleon knew that very well. Furthermore, it is hardly believable that in 1805 a general, even the bravest of the brave, knowing the temperament of his master would dare to take liberties with Napoleon by delivering such a curt repost in this manner.

Be that as it may, Lasalle was attached as brigadier-general to the 1st division of dragoons commanded by General Louis Klein and stayed with this division through the whole campaign of 1805. As is commonly said of this period in his life that, 'it was not his business'. Lasalle the light cavalryman was above all a hussar and his talent lay in the duties of hussars. His name, according to Thoumas, cannot be found in any of the accounts of the campaigns of Ulm and Austerlitz, which suggests he was not active in any principal engagement. This may have been because many of Klein's dragoons were engaged in observation and cordon roles, positioned as a barrier to block the enemy retreat.

At the end of the war, no doubt much to his relief and considerable happiness, Lasalle ceased to be a dragoon and was appointed commander of the light cavalry attached to the 5th Corps d'Armée, that of Lannes, and composed of the Delaage (13th and 21st Chasseurs) and Treilhard brigades (9th and 10th Hussars).

He appears, in this capacity, in a formation of the army in the Battle of Austerlitz; but according to his service, he would not have been invested with this command until December 15th, 1805 thirteen days after the battle took place. In any event he had neither the time nor the opportunity to distinguish himself in this post although it suited him perfectly, and where he found, under his orders his old regiment of the 10th Hussars.

13. The War of the Fourth Coalition 1806-1807

There was little or no intervening period of peace in Europe between the War of the Third Coalition and The War of the Fourth Coalition. Several nations had been continually in conflict with France, which continued to seem irrepressible in the achievement of its ever-developing objectives. Austria had been decisively beaten and now the coalition partners including Prussia, Great Britain, Russia, Saxony and Sweden feared what was to follow as Napoleon's star of good fortune continued to rise. Prussia massed its army in Saxony and Napoleon, in typical style attacked them at lightning speed and inflicted a major defeat upon them at the Battle of Jena-Auerstedt on October 14th, 1806. The French pursued the shattered Prussian forces and occupied Berlin. The war raged on bringing further victories to the French in the battles of Eylau and Friedland, until the Russians called for a truce in 1807.

During the Prussian campaign of 1806, Lasalle's role expanded considerably, and his military talents developed into the securing of commands worthy of him. The general reserve of cavalry had received a new organisation for this campaign. Murat had under his orders the three famous divisions of *cuirassiers* under Nansouty, d'Hautpoul, and Espagne, (the Espagne division only joined the cavalry reserve on the Vistula at the end of December 1806), as well as the five divisions of dragoons under Klein, Beaumont, Grouchy, Sahuc, and Becker. The light cavalry was not undivided; it formed two distinct and independent bri-

10TH HUSSARS

gades: one comprising the 1st Hussars and the 13th Chasseurs under the orders of General Milhaud, the other composed of the 5th and 7th Hussars, 1,200 horses strong, commanded by Lasalle.

These latter two regiments presented a glittering vision on parade as may be imagined since military costume, especially, for the hussars was now at its height in colour and finery. The 5th Hussars were especially vibrantly striking in their bright blue dolmans offset by white pelisses. By contrast, the 7th Hussars presented an opulent, dark ensemble of greens and reds, which showed the golds and yellows on braid and lace to the best possible effect.

Fortunately for Lasalle, both regiments were well served by their officers. The two colonels, Schwartz and Marx, were somewhat elderly, but under their command they had excellent squadron commanders and officers such as Piré, de Brack, and the most remarkable of all, the type of the light cavalry, Curély, who was then *sous-lieutenant* to the *élite* company of the 7th Hussars. All these men would go on to be outstanding commanders of cavalry during the Napoleonic age.

★★★★★★

Thoumas informed his readers, 'For the account of this campaign, the note of Mr. Colonel Lichtenstein, and the work of Capt. Foucart, drawn up from the documents of the Ministry of War, have delivered much valuable information. The manuscript of General Curély was also particularly informative'.

Jean-Nicolas Curély is widely held to be most outstanding light cavalrymen of the First Empire. Indeed, de Brack described him as 'incomparable'. He never saw his full potential realised because he rallied to Napoleon for 'The Hundred Days' and was heartbroken at his master's defeat and fall. He was deprived of his rank in 1824 and he died a comparatively young man in 1827. Hippolyte Piré also rallied to Napoleon in 1815 and fought at Quatre Bras and Waterloo. He survived the campaign, but was exiled

FRENCH HUSSAR TROOPER, 1806

from France by the Bourbon regime, living in Russia and Germany until he was allowed to return in 1819.

✶✶✶✶✶✶

With these two brigades, Napoleon provisionally placed Watier's brigade of light cavalry, attached to the 1st Corps, under Murat's orders to supply the army, and the Grande Duc de Berg (Murat) crossed the German border at the head of six regiments on the 8th October, 1806 (the war had been declared on the 7th October).

On the 9th of October, the Battle of Schleiz, the first serious engagement of the campaign, took place in front of the centre column of the French Army. The Lasalle brigade occupied the right, scouting towards Hof in the east, expanded on a very wide front and took no part. Similarly, Milhaud's brigade was committed to the west towards Saalfeld.

✶✶✶✶✶✶

Édouard Jean-Baptiste Milhaud was commissioned as an officer in 1789 and was a genuine zealot of the revolution, being particularly active politically until the fall of Robespierre. The security of his own head was tenuous for a time, but he was saved by the intercession of the military committee which he had served indisputably well and had thus garnered the support of his colleagues. At this point entirely a soldier, he joined the 5th Dragoons in the Army of Italy.

He supported Bonaparte's *coup d'état* to overthrow the Directory and by 1800 was promoted a general of brigade. He distinguished himself at Jena and Eylau, becoming general of division in 1807. The Peninsular War took him to Spain and Napoleon's Russian folly saw him for a short time military *commandant* of Moscow. Milhaud fought at Leipzig and proved himself to be an exceptional commander of cavalry on the plain of Zeitz in October, 1813. Milhaud rallied to Napoleon for the 'Hundred Days' commanding the IV Cavalry Corps and on June 16th, 1815. It was his *cuirassier* divisions, which broke the Prussian centre

Officer of Hussars, 1805

at Ligny. Much against his protestations and better judgement his cavalry formed part of the great cavalry attack at Waterloo two days afterwards. Unsurprisingly, upon the Bourbon Restoration, Milhaud was exiled as a regicide only being allowed back to France in 1830 following the July Revolution. He died in Aurillac in 1833 aged 67 years.

★★★★★★

The French Army that had entered German territory had been split into three columns and the centre column contained Bernadotte's and Davout's corps supported by some of Murat's cavalry. They first encountered 6,000 Prussians and 3,000 Saxons under the command of Bogislav Tauentzein at Oschitz Wood, south of Schliez. Bernadotte ordered some of his infantry to clear the wood whilst another column, under Drouet, was to advance on Schliez itself. Watier was to follow up with his cavalry. The wood was taken, but progress in that quarter then halted with stiff resistance by the Prussians. However, by two o'clock in the afternoon as the French gathered strength, it became evident to Tauentzein that he could not hold Schliez and he gave orders to withdraw. By late afternoon the town had fallen and Murat's cavalry moved up to press home the victory.

North of Schliez Murat charged the Prussian rear-guard with the 4th Hussars of Watier's brigade, but was repulsed by Prussian cavalry. The 5th Chasseurs à Cheval then came up and, supported by the infantry, the Prussians were push back further to another wooded area to the north of Oettersdorf. A detached enemy unit which had been stationed on the right flank was caught by the French advance as it attempted to rejoin Tauentzein's principal force and was badly mauled.

★★★★★★

Pierre Watier was a consummate cavalry officer of the First Empire of France. He enlisted as a second lieutenant of the 12th Chasseurs à Cheval in 1790, lieutenant of the 16th Chasseurs à Cheval in 1793 and by 1799 he was the colonel of the 4th Dragoons. He was promoted to brigadier-general in December 1805. In keeping with

SENIOR OFFICER OF HUSSARS, 1805

many of his peers he served through most of the principal campaigns of the Napoleonic Wars and he too rallied to Napoleon during the 'Hundred Days' as commander of the 13th Cavalry Division, 4th Cavalry Corps, Army of the North. Unusually, the second Bourbon Restoration only saw him inactive for less than three years since he was called back to the army in 1818 and served in cavalry related senior administrative roles until 1839. He died in 1846.

★★★★★★

The enemy abandoned its position and retreated in good order towards Jena. By the standards of the day this was a minor engagement in which the French force defeated an isolated detachment of the Prussian Army. Napoleon's criticism of Murat's tactics, as a result of this affair, over the excessive dispersion of his cavalry, was classic and for some time was used as a tutorial set piece for officers of cavalry in France.

Following the Battle of Schleiz, the two regiments of Lasalle's brigade continuing their mission to scout and harass the Prussians along their routes, accomplished a particularly long march. On the 11th October, at Gera, they came up to a strongly defended column of caissons and baggage wagons. This was a prize by any standards and Lasalle immediately ordered an attack, which defeated the column's escort troops and resulted in the seizure of 500 caissons and other transport.

The 2nd bulletin of the campaign on this subject confirms this as follows:

> Brigadier General Lasalle, of the reserve cavalry, defeated the escort of the enemy's baggage; 500 caissons and baggage wagons were taken by the hussars, our light cavalry is *"sewn with gold"*; the bridge crews formed part of this convoy; several officers were taken prisoner.

On the following day, the 12th October, Commandant Maignet of the 5th Hussars, once again caught up with the remains of the convoy that had been assaulted on the 11th October, attacked it again and in the course of the fighting captured 25 to 30 men prisoner. Seven wagons and 150 horses were also taken in this engagement. Maignet was wounded in the hand by an enemy officer during close combat, but the hussar was nevertheless able to overcome his opponent whom he killed with his sabre.

Thoumas informed his readers that the hussars of the Lasalle's brigade discovered they were able to operate easily throughout the region at this time by pretending to be Saxon light cavalry; the colours of their *pelisses* and their *dolmans*, but especially those of the trappings, lent themselves very well to this confusion which they did nothing to discourage, until such times as it suited them. Modern readers will discover the likelihood of the success of this ruse by examination of Saxon hussar uniforms, especially compared to those of Lasalle's 5th Hussars, because they are indeed very similar in both colour and appearance, to those of their enemy counterparts.

As early as the 12th October, Lasalle boldly sent mounted raiding parties to Leipzig and Weissenfels. A detachment of fifty hussars under Captain Piré including Sous-Lieutenant Curély among its number entered Leipzig on the 13th October, and captured sixty prisoners, of whom eight were officers. (*Manuscrit de Curély.*)

Lasalle in conference

14. Lasalle's Blunder & Redemption

Lasalle's brigade did not fight on the 14th of October, either at the Battle of Jena or at Auerstedt. On the 15th October it was summoned to present itself before Erfurt, but it departed that place without waiting for the capitulation of the town.

After marching all day on the 16th October, the brigade joined on the 17th October with Klein's dragoon division, on the road which followed Blücher with his retiring Prussian columns to Tönnstadt near Weissensee. Here it was alleged that Lasalle allowed himself to be duped by Blücher in parley, because the old general convinced him that a six-week armistice had just been concluded, and since that was the case, he reasoned, Lasalle should allow his force unimpeded passage without confrontation. The allegation was that Lasalle simply took Blücher at his word on the matter and so, indeed, allowed the Prussian column go its way unmolested.

Of course, it transpired this claim of Blücher's was completely untrue and thus, it was said, Lasalle had been fooled by a simple unverified lie. To make matters worse Klein allegedly fell for exactly the same trick with the same outcome at Weissensee. Napoleon upon hearing of these incidents was furious, mindful no doubt that the actions of the buffoon by implication travel upwards to taint the buffoon's master and all his works. This, beyond the simple matter of personal humiliation, has tangible tactical advantages and disadvantages in terms of morale. Both officers were accordingly severely blamed by the Emperor's order of October 19th, 1806. Napoleon was not inclined to forgive his generals errors of judgement in these kinds of circumstances and did hold back the vehemence of his admonishments.

> The Emperor testifies his dissatisfaction to General of Division Klein and General of Brigade Lasalle, and His Majesty orders that this mark of his dissatisfaction be placed at the command of the army, for having allowed two enemy columns which were cut off, to pass, both of whom had the extreme simplicity of believing what the enemy general, Blücher had told and written them. Since when is it that His Majesty passes his orders through the channel of the enemy?

There are usually two sides to every story and so there was another version of the incident which showed Lasalle's conduct in a better light. Lasalle, marching with his brigade, had scarcely 700 to 800 fighting men at this time at his disposal. At a certain point he was informed by his scouts that he had before him a column of 6,000 cavalry and 10,000 infantry blocking his own line of march. At this point his options were limited and the best outcome possible would be one where his command was not annihilated.

> However, irrespective of the facts of the matter when Lasalle heard of the Emperor's condemnation of his conduct so publicly announced, the shame of it provoked him to consider blowing his brains out. His officers, of course, prevented him from taking such an impetuous course of action and escorted him to Napoleon, who accepted his explanations, but, as usual, did not rescind his order of the day since to do so would have demonstrated a fallibility which emperors prefer to give the impression they do not possess. (*Manuscrit de Curély*.)

Following this incident Lasalle vowed to make the Prussians pay dearly for his discomfort and redoubled his ardour in pursuing them. After several days in which he accomplished marches of forty-five, fifty-five, and sixty kilometres each and sent recon-

PLAN OF STETTIN

naissance in all directions, he arrived at Oranienburg on the 25th of October. There he ascertained that the Prince of Hohenlohe, with 18,000 men, was marching from Magdeburg to Stettin, and that the King of Prussia had gone to Oranienburg, on his way to Custrin. On the way, on the 24th, Lasalle had, according to Thoumas, subjugated the citadel of Spandau, whose governor was to surrender the next day to the infantry of Marshal Lannes.

On the morning of the 26th October he departed at Murat's command for Zehdenick, where his own vanguard reached the rear-guard of the Prussian Army. Fourteen enemy squadrons, among them the Black Hussars and the Queen's Dragoons were in line of battle behind Zehdenick. After several partially successful charges, Lasalle united the squadrons he had under his command, that is, about 300 hussars, and, according to Murat in his report to the Emperor, did good work to hold the enemy until the arrival of Grouchy's division of dragoons, which had followed him closely. Then he made a move towards the enemy's position and observing that manoeuvres were being undertaken to surround him, he immediately ordered a charge.

The hussars, according to the testimony of Murat, charged on 'with the rapidity of lightning', defeated everything in their path, drove out the Prussian cavalry from the city, threw it in chaos into a defile, and pursued it for more than a league allowing no opportunity for it to rally.

Lasalle says in his report:

> The Colonel of the Régiment de la Reine (Queen's Dragoons), the Major of the *Hussars de Schimmelpfennig*, and almost all the officers and 600 men were killed or taken. The standard of the *Régiment de la Reine* fell into the hands of my hussars. At the end of the defile, the hussars, exhausted with fatigue, threw themselves on the right of the road, to allow the dragoons to charge in their turn, or rather, to tell the truth, the hussars having passed the wood, met with fresh troops which brought them back with sufficient force and were definitively defeated by the dragoons under Grouchy. (*Manuscrit de Curély.*)

Murat wrote to the Emperor:

> Your cavalry has really covered itself with glory, General Lasalle has quite erased the day of Weissensee.

It should be added that Lasalle had covered 28 kilometres with his brigade before fighting for several hours. Yet he apparently did not yet regard himself as sufficiently avenged for his humiliation and soon on the 27th October, he marched on Prenzlow (Prenzlau), and occupying the heights which dominate the city, he launched his squadrons into the suburbs just at the moment when the enemy troops of the Prince de Hohenlohe were entering it by another road.

Murat said in a new letter:

> The two heads of column arrived together to this city, the hussars must have done the honours and let the Prussian column pass.

More accurately, Schwerin's *cuirassiers* pushed Lasalle's light cavalry aside. Murat attempted to persuade the Prussian commander to surrender by the deception that besides his own force which he claimed amounted to 30,000 men, Lannes was rapidly approaching at the head of 60,000 more French troops ready to join the action. On this occasion the French herald was sent packing with a refusal.

Murat, with the boldness for which he was renowned, immediately ordered the attack. Lasalle galloped towards the town, followed by Grouchy's dragoons. Supported by a battery of light artillery, Lasalle over threw everything before him, whilst the dragoons under Grouchy turned to take the enemy in the flank. Eventually, and after another refusal to surrender, believing himself to be pressed on all sides with no possible chance of extricating his force the Prince of Hohenlohe at this point resigned himself to capitulation and laid down the arms of 17 battalions of infantry and 19 squadrons of cavalry. It was Hohenlohe's turn to be the victim of an audacious bluff and the recourse of trickery, rather than musketry had not yet run its course in this campaign. The demoralised prince was eventually persuaded his situation was hopeless when in fact only Murat's cavalry and a brigade of French infantry were in his immediate vicinity.

On this incident, it is stated in the records of Lasalle:

Cited, in an agenda of the Emperor, as having powerfully contributed, from the beginning of the Prussian campaign, to the capture of several generals, Hohenlohe, Prince Augustus of Prussia, Prince Schwerin, 16,000 infantry, 6 regiments of cavalry, and 64 pieces of cannon.

The day after Prenzlow's surrender, the Emperor wrote to Prince Murat:

Show my satisfaction to the dragoons and light cavalry of Milhaud and Lasalle.

But Napoleon was soon to learn of a more extraordinary feat of arms for which Lasalle was responsible. On the very day when he congratulated the light cavalry for extremes of valour, Lasalle presented himself with his brigade before the fortress of Stettin. The cannon of the place having shot some hopeful balls in his direction, he ordered his regiments to be concentrated in a sheltered position. He ordered his men to build and ignite more campfires than were required to give the impression that his force was considerably larger than was actually the case. Meanwhile two officers went on his behalf to summon the governor of Stettin to surrender.

At two o'clock in the morning, these two officers returned with the capitulation document signed. The garrison was to march out at eight o'clock on to the glacis and be made prisoners of war. Lasalle immediately informed Murat and asked him for infantry to provide the necessary support for the operation, but at the appointed hour none of the expected troops had yet arrived, with the exception of a single regiment supported by two cannons.

Seeing at once that they were dealing with so few people to ensure their cooperation, the Prussian troops pretended to revolt as a pretext to effect an escape. Without losing a moment, Lasalle had them charged by his hussars and scattered them across the plain. The arrival of Victor returning with the infantry of Marshal Lannes, put an end to the business, and 'rid of this chore,' said Lasalle, 'I was able to continue my journey.'

It was on this occasion that Napoleon memorably wrote to Murat:

> If your hussars are able to take strongholds, I have only to dissolve my great artillery, and to dismiss my genius.

★★★★★★

The old General Friedrich von Romberg, who commanded at the fortress of Stettin and who was thus comprehensively tricked out of defensive works and who put his name to the capitulation, 'gave as a gift' to Lasalle, as a token of his 'esteem' according to Thoumas, a superb Turkish pipe enriched with gem stones. It is this pipe that Lasalle has at his feet in the beautiful portrait of him painted by the artist, Antoine-Jean Gros, a pupil of David, who was responsible for several of the famous paintings of the revolution, consulate and empire periods including the magnificent portrait of Napoleon Bonaparte mounted upon a rearing white charger at the crossing of the Alps.

Romberg predictably paid dearly for his error and his 'esteem' for Lasalle, because he was tried by a Prussian military tribunal for surrendering Stettin without resistance, found guilty and sentenced to life in imprisonment. Elderly, frail and disgraced he died in Berlin before he was able to take up his sentence, aged 80 years. However, it was acquired, Romberg's pipe became emblematic of General Lasalle's appearance for the remainder of his life and indeed for posterity.

★★★★★★

Lasalle continued his march on Damm, Anklam, Schwerin and Lübeck, by forty and fifty-five-kilometre journeys. According to Thoumas, Lasalle took an active part in the Battle of Lübeck, on the 6th of November, 1806 though it is Watier's brigade that is recorded in this battle. Certainly, thereafter the French had Blücher 'on the run' and within a circling movement enveloped his exhausted command at Radtkau where he was compelled, out of options, to surrender to the three marshals—Bernadotte, Soult and Murat.

Blücher to conclude the matter wrote a curt note thus:

> I capitulate since I have neither bread nor ammunition. Signed, BLÜCHER.

Few incidents in military history as it applies to cavalry can equal the enterprise and ardour with which Lasalle and his hussars pursued the remains of the Prussian Army during this campaign. According to many accounts, it was this outstanding performance which earned Lasalle's brigade the undeniably evocative sobriquet, 'The Infernal Brigade'. It must be noted that Thoumas in his account does not mention this appellation at all, which is noteworthy in as much as one would imagine, given its peculiar singularity, it would be unlikely to be overlooked by any historian.

15. Lasalle: General of Division, 1806–1808

Now that the Prussian Army had been decisively beaten Napoleon turned his attention to the east towards his nearest and mightiest enemy, Russia. Between where his armies stood and those of the enemy lay Poland, a country begrudgingly labouring under the oppressive yoke of Russia and receptive to measures that might relieve them of it. Accordingly, the emperor ordered the Grand Army to march towards the Vistula.

From October 7th to November 7th, 1806, the Lasalle Brigade had marched every day at an average of forty-two kilometres, and double that total on certain occasions. On the 7th of November, it was on its way back to Berlin, where it had passed in revue before the Emperor on the 21st of November. On the 28th of November, Murat entered into Warsaw at the head of the advanced guard to cheers of enthusiastic joy from the Poles who looked upon the French Army and its master as the means by which the Polish Kingdom might at last be restored.

Alas, in this they were mistaken for Napoleon's seduction on the subject was one more of his great betrayals of statecraft. There could not be a world wherein he could afford to permanently alienate the Russian *Tsar* and this the emperor knew well. He had no intention of facilitating the recreation of a Polish nation, though he predictably took advantage of the tide of nationalist sentiment that swept the country to embrace into his armies, significant numbers of Polish troops among which were the deservedly renowned Polish cavalryman who multiplied their existing fame by faithfully serving under French imperial banners and spending their lives in a tragically futile cause.

By the 5th of December, Lasalle's hussars were bivouacking near Warsaw and on the 19th of that month, Napoleon entered the Polish capital bringing with him an army of 120,000 men.

★★★★★★

The cavalry of the First Empire has often been reproached for the rapid using up of its mounts.

The number of horses actually only decreased in Lasalle's command from 7th October to 15th November, 1806 by only 244 mounts out of a total of 1,242. It is true, however, that the regiments of cavalry had risen on more than one occasion to full strength in mounts, not entirely as a consequence of their own animal husbandry, but rather at the expense of the enemy as a consequence of the introduction of newly captured cavalry mounts.

Captain Foucart, in *Campagne de Prusse* stated with some authority:

'The cavalry of the first Empire used up its horses when it was badly conducted.'

Thoumas countered not unreasonably:

'What could be said, for example, of the brigade of Auguste Colbert, attached to the corps of Marshal Ney, leaving Silesia in August 1808, marching without loss of a mount to Madrid in Spain, and then pursuing the English Army, forming the advanced guard of Marshal Soult, and only stopping on the 11th of January, 1809, at La Coruña, on the Atlantic shore?'

★★★★★

Irrespective of the lateness of the year, Napoleon immediately ordered advances which would provoke an engagement with the Russians, who manoeuvred in dreadful wet weather, which turned the unmetalled roads of Poland to quagmires, which hindered the progress of both armies. The weather became master of the campaign to the degree that the French artillery frequently lagged behind the marching and mounted columns and this

was to significantly affect the next engagement in which Lasalle and his men would fight, for the French artillery was thus entirely prevented from taking part in it. The Russians retreated and advanced until the 26th of December when Benningsen, defying orders to once again retire, elected to stand and fight the French at Pultusk.

Meanwhile on the same day, to the north-west, Golitsyn's 4th Division and Dokhturov's 5th Division were retreating to Ostrolenka *via* the town of Golymin where, exhausted, the Russian troops paused to rest. Murat's cavalry and Augereau's 7th Corps marched out towards the enemy in the early morning of the 26th and Lasalle, in typical fashion, ensured that his division was first to sight the enemy at 10 o'clock that morning. A Russian two squadron cavalry rear-guard, which was quickly reinforced by three further squadrons of *cuirassiers* forced Lasalle's men back into the woods from which they had debouched, but by 2 o'clock in the afternoon the French infantry appeared on the field and marched to engage the enemy, though it made little progress.

Murat also attacked with Klein's, Milhaud's and Davout's cavalry and had some small success before they were neutralised by the terrain, the weather and stubborn resistance. Move and counter move by both sides failed to bring about a decisive outcome the engagement and the early falling darkness terminated fighting and enabled the Russians to withdraw in good order. We are told that General of Brigade, Jacques Marguerite Étienne de Fornier (also known as 'Fénerolz') was killed by the shell of a howitzer at the head of his brigade comprising the 1st and 2nd Dragoons of Klein's division whilst coming to the aid of Lasalle and his brigade during this battle. The battle at Golymin, like Pultusk, was an inconclusive affair. The Russians withdrew leaving the field to the French who entered Golymin on the morning of the 27th of December, 1806.

Golymin was a small battle by the standards of Napoleonic warfare, but it had particular significance for General Lasalle, because in it his cavalry fell prey to extraordinary disaster which

Lasalle and Murat at the Battle of Heilsberg, June 10, 1807

held the potential to irreparably damage his reputation and that of his brigade. Receiving the order to charge the Russian artillery, the 5th and 7th Hussars, who had neither infantry nor cavalry before them, had moved to advance when they heard someone shouting the order, '*Halt*'. This cry, which was naturally assumed by the troopers to emanate from an officer who had the authority to issue it, was repeated throughout the line. At once the squadrons broke up and retreated in such disorder that they could not be rallied until a quarter of an hour had elapsed. Lasalle, who had been leading the charge, had discovered his isolation, turned about and returned to his lines. We may only imagine his emotions.

It seems sober common sense to imagine that a brigade with the confirmed *élan*, experience and reputation as the one that Lasalle commanded (and particularly since it was Lasalle who commanded it) would be highly unlikely to unilaterally retreat on a field of battle, unless it was in the presence of forces of crushing superiority. So, the panic (if such it was), which seized it in the Battle of Golymin, may therefore, be cited as a proof that the most solid troops are themselves subject to inexplicable failures.

★★★★★★

Students of military history will note this incident bears a remarkable similarity with that of the 14th Light Dragoons of the British Army in India during the Second Sikh War at the Battle of Chillianwallah in 1849. Once again, an unauthorised order threw an advance into chaos causing a *volte-face* as the regiment was in the act of closing with the enemy. In these circumstances, aspersions are inevitably levelled at the rank and file, though it is more the case that troops are drilled to act immediately without question upon orders and when those go awry, lose focus until order is restored by officers in whom they have faith. Predictably, blame inevitably falls upon the shoulders of those who are powerless to defend their honour, for given the positive or negative outcome of any situation the troops suffer condemnation upon disobeying an order and equally when they believe they are obeying one.

✶✶✶✶✶✶

When the brigade was again assembled, Lasalle had it brought forward, and held it in formation through two hours of darkness, standing motionless under the enemy's cannon fire where, as a consequence, it suffered the regrettable losses of ten men and eleven horses killed. The general himself had two horses killed under him. At the end of two hours Lasalle ordered, 'Break the Ranks' to bring to an end the punishment.

The next day the two regimental colonels were appointed *généraux de brigade* (generals of brigade), retired from active service, and replaced by two strong *chefs de corps*. These were Colonels Déry, *aide-de-camp* of Murat who, having become General, was killed at the Battle of Winkowo during the campaign to Russia, and Édouard Colbert (Pierre David Édouard de Colbert-Chabanais), who soon became one of the most brilliant cavalry divisionaries. (*Manuscrit de Curély*.)

✶✶✶✶✶✶

As with so many of the outstanding cavalrymen who have appeared in these pages, Colbert fought with distinction through the revolutionary wars, in Egypt and during the conflicts of the First Empire. Notably, he was wounded at Wagram like Lasalle, shot in the head, without suffering fatal results! He initially prevaricated about rejoining Napoleon during the Hundred Days and when he eventually decided to join his master, Napoleon scolded him icily upon his arrival by saying, 'Colbert, I have been waiting for you for three days,' to which Colbert allegedly replied, 'I have been waiting for you for a year!' Colbert fought at Waterloo where he was wounded and though initially disgraced by the Bourbon Restoration, served again in the army in the first expedition to Constantine, North Africa in 1836.

✶✶✶✶✶✶

The lapse of discipline among the hussars at Golymin was

Lasalle and Murat at Heilsberg,

demonstrably not charged as a crime against General Lasalle personally, because he was promoted on the 30th of December to the rank of *général de division*. All the light cavalry of the reserve of this army was then united under his orders. It formed a superb division of three brigades, each comprising three regiments with usually three squadrons each and commanded by the Generals La Tour-Maubourg, Bruyère and Watier.

Modern readers may consider that Lasalle was exceptionally hard upon his men for the incident at Golymin and his response to it more than draconian. However, these were times when considerations of 'honour' took precedence in the minds of many over all other things and to his credit, Lasalle stood with his men throughout their ordeal under fire in shared responsibility, which was intended to regain the honour of the brigade and to importantly demonstrate to the army that his brigade, whatever its aberrational shortcomings and beyond the need for further debate or speculation, contained no cowards.

★★★★★★

Whilst they had recently been colleagues and generals of brigade, Lasalle was now the superior officer of General Watier and apparently this did not sit well with the subordinate.

So much is evident from the tone of his surviving correspondence of the period, which was addressed to Lasalle. 'I see, General,' Watier wrote to his new division commander on January 2nd, 1807, 'that, having not had the honour of waging war with you, we are entirely foreign to you. What has happened up to this point is that I received my orders directly from the Prince Murat!' (Letter quoted by Captain Foucart, *Campagne de Pologne*)

Subordinates do, irrespective of their feelings on the matter, have to accept the new status of officers who have recently been colleagues and since that is the case, the transition may as well be undertaken with good grace. This short note makes it clear that Watier was unable to manage that simple obligation to Lasalle and we may speculate why this was the case. The fact is that most of the significant light cavalry battlefield activity had in this campaign been shouldered thus far, with some notable success, by Watier's brigade and so, irrelevant though it was, Watier had been receiving orders from Murat directly. It is entirely possible that this communication was simply an expression of 'sour grapes' from an officer who believed that if the laurels of promotion were to be given at this time that they should be given to him. Nevertheless, early insubordination does not auger well for harmonious cooperation at a later date and General Watier was soon, perhaps predictably, to be replaced by General Durosnel, and Pajol replaced La Tour-Maubourg, as general of the division after the battle of February 5th, 1807

★★★★★★

Two of the nine regiments in the division had four squadrons, bringing the total number of squadrons to thirty-eight and the division's strength to more than 5,700 men and horses. During the time it spent in winter quarters, in consequence of the campaign of Poland, it was placed in front of Marshal Soult's corps.

The *Bulletin de la Grande Armée* says:

> On the 4th of February, at daybreak, the General of light cavalry, Lasalle, defeated all the enemy upon the plain with his hussars. A line of Cossacks and other enemy cavalry came immediately before him; He marched to the enemy, who fought for six hours; the enemy's cavalry was overthrown several times.

> On the 5th of February, the Emperor sent the cavalry including Lasalle's division to Marshal Ney. Lasalle, with his usual vigour, repulsed a corps of 1500 cavalry, who wished to oppose his march, and seized the enemy's depots and stores. Then under Marshal Ney's command he took part in the Battle of Kreutzberg, which was delivered to the rear of the force under the Prussian general, Lestocq.

This engagement is so rarely reported that a passage from a

book written by an English tourist, Richard Bryan Smith, who visited the site of the battle in 1818, is fascinating, so worthy of inclusion though, regrettably, no reference is made to the activities of the French cavalry. Given the pedigree of this account no guarantees can be made concerning its accuracy.

> On the 22nd of July we left Königsberg for Kreutzberg, 3¾ miles, Prussian Eylau, 2¾ miles. The latter town has 1600 inhabitants, and near it runs a small stream, discharging itself into the *Frische Haff,* at Brandenburg; upon it there is a castle of the Teutonic Knights, in ruins. The desperate battle fought near this place, on the 8th of February, 1807, was of great importance, and, on the whole, would have been favourable to the Allies, had they been able immediately to follow up the advantage they certainly gained. The country in the immediate neighbourhood is open, and the land in general level, excepting a few ridges, occasionally rising to a moderate height.
> Our guide had been a trumpeter in the action; but his story was rather confused, and he was continually reverting to his own prowess. He said that skirmishing commenced at Grünhafge, some miles distant, and that the Russians, who were in possession of the town, planted their cannon on a small elevation to the eastward.
> Napoleon took his station in the steeple of the church: it is built of wood, and covered with shingles, through which holes were made for him to observe the progress of the contest: and the precise spot on which he stood was carefully pointed out to us by our guide. As the steeple was perforated in several places by bullets, the person of Napoleon must have been in considerable danger.
> The place was plainly marked by gentle undulations of the earth, where the bodies of a number of brave fellows had been laid, particularly those, we were told of the French artillery, many of whom were drowned in attempting to bring their guns over a neighbouring piece of water, which was frozen, but not sufficiently strong to bear heavy

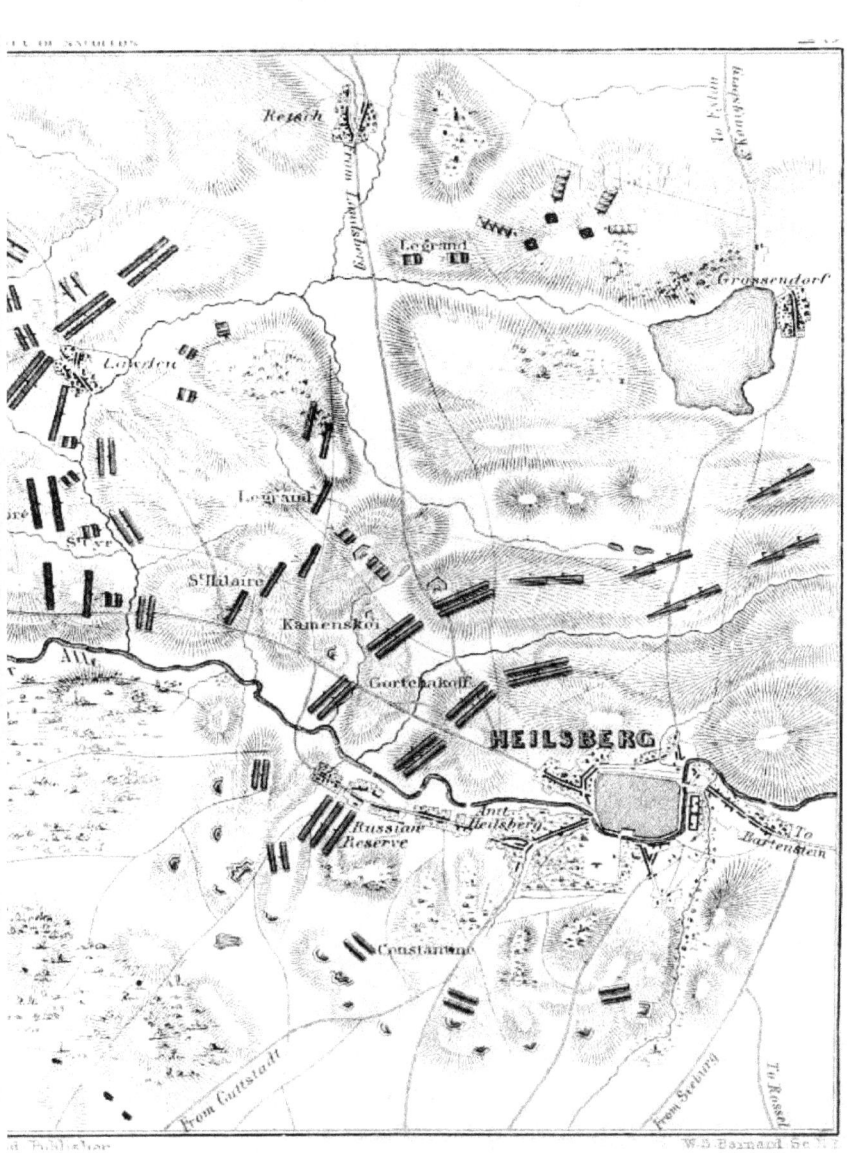

carriages.

The troops had been engaged six hours before General Benningsen, the Russian commander-in-chief, joined them; and for fourteen hours the brave Russians sustained the desperate fire of the French artillery, without support, as it was late in the evening ere the Prussians, under General Lestocq, made their appearance. They decided the day; but Napoleon was suffered to retire unmolested, and take up a position on the River Passarge, which he did not leave until he marched in triumph to Königsberg.

We proceeded, through a fine and well-cultivated country, to Landsberg, 2; Mehlsack, 4; Mühlhausen, 4 miles. Between the latter places we crossed the Passarge, the approach to which had been defended by Napoleon by a strong battery of eight guns and a *tête du pont;* and on the road we could distinctly trace the route of the French Army. (Richard Bryan Smith. *Notes made during a tour of Denmark, Holstein etc)*

Lasalle's cavalry next preceded the 6th Corps on to the battlefield of Eylau, assuring its outlet to the village of Althof, where Lasalle set up his bivouac on the evening of the battle. He was then ordered, under Murat, to Königsberg in pursuit of the Russian Army, and took up a position two leagues from that city. Attached again to Marshal Ney's corps on 16th February to cover the retreat with his division, he was able to repulse all the attempts made by the enemy against the rear-guard and took an active part in the fighting of the 3rd March, 1807.

The French Army had, by this time effectively settled in winter quarters along a line from Warsaw to Elbing, making good use of the rivers Vistula, Wkra and Narew. The appalling weather made tactical movement ponderous to the point of ineffectuality and this consideration was compounded in Napoleon's mind by his inability to determine in which direction his enemy might next manoeuvre.

Meanwhile the war continued practically where it could. Dantzig was besieged, Prince Jerome invested the strongholds in

Silesia and Sebastiani collaborated with the Turks to fortify the Dardanelles to disadvantage the Royal Navy.

At the resumption of hostilities at the beginning of June 1807, Lasalle, whose division had been brought up to four brigades and had been sent back to Elbing, had the opportunity of displaying all his strength in the Battle of Guttstadt, where light cavalry regiments of his division pursued and hard pressed the enemy as far as Deppen. In fact, the engagement is principally known as Guttstadt-Deppen.

After the terrible conflict of Eylau Benningsen had taken position at Heilsberg and there established a strongly entrenched camp. The French brought battle to the stubborn, well placed, disciplined and powerfully armed Russians who defended it on the following day, June 10th.

In this battle, 'so imprudently engaged by Murat and Soult' (as Thoumas informs us, though Napoleon and Berthier were present) French troops dashed themselves against these strong redoubts and, though the struggle was terrible, failed to take them. Benningsen, however, fearing he would be cut off evacuated the position during the night and marching down the bank of the River Alle, on the 13th June reached Friedland, which on the following day was destined to be another memorable scene of carnage.

Lasalle's division of light cavalry at Heilsberg consisted of some 2,700 troops. Pajol's brigade consisted of the 5th and 7th Hussars, together with the 3rd Chasseurs à Cheval. Durousnel's brigade contained the 7th, 20th and 22nd Chasseurs à Cheval and Watier commanded a brigade consisting of the 11th Chasseurs à Cheval, the 2nd Bavarian Chevau-légers and the Württemberg Chevau-légers.

The French cavalry, launched by Murat with, as usual, more audacity than timidity, had to sustain itself through several lively engagements and one of them has provided an account of Lasalle in action which has become one of the most often recounted events of his colourful career. Colonel de Gonneville recounts details in his *Souvenirs*. After explaining that the division of Espagne's *cuirassiers*, of which he was a part, was in front of sixty Russian squadrons with a great disadvantage in terms of the terrain, he added:

> At this moment, the Grande Duc de Berg (Murat) arrived from the rear of our right, followed by his staff and galloped near our front, lying on the neck of his horse, and foiled any chance of discourse on the part of General Espagne, passing very quickly before him before moving rapidly away. The only word I heard was, "*Charge!*"
>
> This order, given without any other qualification, was directed at fifteen unsupported squadrons to launch an attack upon sixty elite squadrons, seemed to me the more difficult to explain than approve, because, in order to join with the enemy, it was necessary for the charge to cross over an almost impassable ravine. This could only be achieved by the troopers in small broken numbers, after which they were required to form again under the fire of the enemy two hundred paces in advance of their original line.

★★★★★★

Gonneville, a Norman noble, had begun his career in 1804 as a *chasseur* with the 20th regiment, but was principally a heavy cavalry officer serving throughout the period as a *cuirassier*. He fought in the brutal 'war to the knife' against Spanish guerillas as well as at Eylau, Somosierra, Königsberg and other engagements.

★★★★★★

By means of contrast Commandant Parquin, (the author of one of the most well-known chronicles concerning the French light cavalry, during the Napoleonic era that has been translated in English) who was then *maréchal des logis* in the 20th Chasseurs was escorting Murat that day. He noted that his superb, if impulsive, master of cavalry, whilst passing at the *triple gallop* next to the 5th regiment of Hussars, shouted to Colonel Déry, his former *aide-de-camp*, these brief words: 'Follow me with your regiment,' and then threw himself with typical courage into the *mêlée.* (*Revue de cavalerie,* October 1885.)

Lasalle's division fought with admirable fierceness, and, according to Curély with his usual talent for understatement, '*made good charges*'.

Murat, who had his horse killed under him and had remounted himself by commandeering that of a brigadier of the 20th Chasseurs, was at one point surrounded by a dozen or so Russian dragoons in the thick of the fighting and was certainly about to be imminently killed or taken prisoner. Lasalle, perceiving the danger Murat was facing, rushed towards him and extricated him from the *mêlée.*

Confirmation of his actions on this occasion is found in a mention within General Lasalle's service record. A biographer adds that an instant afterwards Lasalle in his turn found himself surrounded by the enemy and in much the same position that Murat was in when he saved him. In moments he was delivered from danger by Murat personally, who embraced him, held out his hand and said to him: 'We are quits, my dear General.'

On the 11th, at daybreak, Lasalle's division repulsed the Russian cavalry. It formed Murat's vanguard in his march on Königsberg and Tilsit, and had several remarkable engagements, including that of the 16th of June at Taplacker, where by the precision of his manoeuvres and the strength of his attacks on the enemy line, Lasalle dispersed a large group of Cossacks, and, after a most lively battle, he also put to flight the Russian infantry. He continued the course of his successes on the 17th and 18th and entered Tilsit on the morning of the 19th of June. (*Le général Pajol, Histoire de Pajol,* t. II.)

When, after the peace of Tilsit, the Lasalle division was reviewed by the Emperor it comprised (according to Thoumas) 5,400 horses in the ranks.

It has been said that Lasalle, upon being appointed *Grand-officier de la Légion d'honneur* and *Comte de l'Empire,* complained to Napoleon that he had not been placed 'at the head of the most beautiful regiment in the world,' meaning the *Chasseurs à Cheval de la Garde,* to replace Colonel Dahlmann, who had been killed at the Battle of Eylau, and the Emperor replied:

> When General Lasalle will no longer smoke and swear, I shall call him my chamberlain.

This anecdote may be true, but General Lasalle was not appointed as Grand-Officer of the Legion of Honour and count of the empire at this period of 1807. He actually received the grand-officer's award fifteen months later. On September 4th, 1808, following his victory at the Battle of Medina de Rio Seco in Spain. The title of 'Count' was conferred on him in the same year together with an endowment of 50,000 *francs*, or rather more accurately, two endowments of 25,000 *francs* each.

One of Lasalle's friends, General Fournier, was one of the most brilliant officers of French light cavalry next to Montbrun. He later demonstrated his talents at the Battle of Fuentes de Oñoro, 1811 during the Peninsular War where at the head of his brigade of *Chasseurs à Cheval* he, according to Thoumas, achieved the no mean feat of allegedly breaking into three squares of British infantry and wreaking havoc within them. The present writer has not been able to verify this remarkable claim, though is aware of the notable effectiveness of infantry in square against French cavalry in this battle. (See Appendix.) Previously at Lugo during May, 1809 in north-western Spain, he had successfully defended the town with a force of just 1,500 men against an attacking Spanish Army of 15,000 men under Mahy.

★★★★★★

Despite his undisputed qualities as a soldier, François Fournier-Sarlovèze (as he became ultimately known after the Bourbon Restoration) was infamously known as 'the worst subject in the *Grande Armée*' and such was his distinction that he became the inspiration for one of the principal characters in Joseph Conrad's fictional story, *The Duel* which was also made into a motion picture directed by Ridley Scott as, 'The Duellists'. The other protagonist was in reality Pierre Dupont de l'Étang who had the misfortune of being ordered to deliver a disagreeable message to Fournier which, enraging him, resulted in the issuing of a series of challenges, which became so out of control that it is said the pair fought thirty duels with each other protracted over a period of many years. The affair only came to end when, in a duel with pistols, Dupont having Fournier at a fatal disadvantage forced him to promise to henceforth leave him alone.

Fournier was, in fact, an incorrigible hothead constantly in trouble for duelling, financial transgressions, assaults and absenting himself without leave. All these irregularities perpetually resulted in arrests, suspensions, and actual imprisonments. In Lasalle, however, he found a like-minded confederate who was ready and able to approve of practically any escapade. Lasalle could, above all be depended upon to support a light cavalry officer whose aggressive propensities would make him invaluable upon the field of battle. It may have appealed to Lasalle that, in Fournier there was an even more outrageous example of the 'light cavalry officer type' than he was himself. It is a matter of record that he faithfully supported Fournier through the consequences of his self-inflicted misfortunes by pleading his case with Napoleon for years who, invariably, out of regard for Lasalle, eventually pardoned Fournier for his latest misbehaviour.

However, it was inevitable that Fournier's excesses would never be tolerated by the emperor indefinitely, despite the constant persuasions of his loyal advocate during his lifetime. Lasalle's demise in 1809 and thus the curtailing of his moderating patronage did nothing to assuage Fournier's lack of discipline and so he continued to find himself regularly admonished and out of favour. Although he was appointed a Count of the Empire in 1813 he was shortly deprived of his rank following an insubordinate verbal altercation with Napoleon. The emperor went so far on this occasion as to send Fournier to Mayence Prison for displaying 'a defeatist attitude' following the reverse at Leipzig.

Astonishingly, on his way to his cell his carriage and escort of *Gendarmes* were attacked by Cossacks and Fournier, taking a sword from the corpse a dead trooper, led the assault and routed the Russians. He then regained his seat in his carriage and ordered, 'Onwards to Mayence!'

Fournier did not rally to Napoleon during the Hundred Days period showing, it has to be noted, an entirely uncharacteristic circumspection of the matter of the potentials of Napoleon's success.

★★★★★★

After the peace, General Lasalle passed with his division, reduced to two brigades, to the 3rd *Corps de la Grande-Armée*, under the orders of Davout, August 1, 1807; his headquarters were in Warsaw. At the end of the year he was recalled to organise a cavalry division at Poitiers destined to be part of the Army of Spain and on 18 February, 1808 he was appointed *commandant* of the cavalry reserve of this army.

16. War in the Iberian Peninsula, 1808

The cavalry division formed at Poitiers, which was supposed to be composed of provisional regiments, received on the contrary, established regiments with renowned service records, including the 10th Chasseurs à Cheval, the fine reputation of which dated from the campaign of 1796 in Italy. Among its colonels had been Ordener and Auguste Colbert, and it had distinguished itself at the battles of Gradisca, Messkirch, Elchingen and Jena. Another welcome addition was the 22nd Chasseurs à Cheval, which Lasalle had commanded during the Egyptian Campaign and which had been so well regarded by the remainder of the army in North Africa.

★★★★★★

Auguste Colbert, incidentally, was famously, at the Battle of Cacabelos in Spain, to fall victim to the superlative marksmanship of Rifleman, Thomas Plunket of the 95th Rifles who killed him with a single shot at extreme long range with his Baker rifle when Colbert had every reason to imagine he was safe from the discharge of an enemy personal weapon. With his next shot, Plunket then shot and killed the French officer who had come to Colbert's aid.

★★★★★★

At the end of April, 1808, this division was marching *en route* to Bayonne in the south of France, from whence it was to serve as an escort to Napoleon as he entered Spain. Rapidly developing political events in Spain decided otherwise.

On February 16th, 1808 under the pretext of re-enforcing French troops engaged in Portugal under Junot, Napoleon had invaded Spain. The French occupied Pamplona in the north before moving on to Barcelona on the east coast. On March 19th King Charles IV of Spain was forced to abdicate his throne and four days later a French Army led by Murat marched into the Spanish capital, Madrid.

A popular insurrection against French occupation broke out in Madrid on the 2nd of May 1808. The uprising culminated in a fierce battle in the central square of the Puerta del Sol where the Spanish insurgents were decisively crushed. Murat ordered hundreds of citizens shot that night along the Prado promenade in reprisal. Paintings and sketches of executions of Spanish civilians by the artist, Goya have immortalised these atrocities. On June 15th Napoleon placed his brother, Joseph on the throne of Spain and the country became a battleground. The Peninsular War had begun and would rage on until 1814. For the French, draining effects 'the Spanish Ulcer' would ultimately spell disaster.

Eventually, a British Army would land to assist in expelling the French from Spain and that campaign would bring forth one of the finest generals that nation had ever produced who would eventually become, on the muddy slopes of Belgium beyond Waterloo, Napoleon's nemesis. Lasalle would never face the red coated soldiers who marched and fought for Wellington, for his own war in Spain would be confined to fighting the Spanish themselves.

★★★★★★★★★★★★

In addition to the corps sent to Portugal under Junot, a second and a third had entered Spain, commanded by Dupont and Marshal Moncey respectively. Marshal Bessières was invested with the command of the troops assembled under the name of *Corps des Pyrénées Occidentales*, (Corps of the Western Pyrenees), which comprised the two infantry divisions of Merle and Verdier. The Lasalle cavalry division was attached to this army corps, charged with occupying the north of Spain.

Having scarcely marched into Spain beyond the mountains of the Pyrenees, Lasalle was ordered to move onwards to Valladolid, deep in the interior, with a column of four battalions. His seven hundred cavalrymen of the 10th and 22nd Chasseurs à Cheval accompanied by six guns, were charged with the responsibility to forcibly disperse all Spanish insurgents in their path, which had been assembled with intent to impede the passage of the army. Lasalle's command marched south followed at a distance by the infantry division under Merle.

Lasalle's mixed command left the city of Burgos on June 5th travelling south-west and arriving in front of the village of Torquemada, on the night on the June 6th. There, Lasalle discovered an 800-metre low, stone bridge over the River Pisuerga which was barriered with chains and carts and held defensively by a force of armed civilians. Lasalle's vanguard, composed of a company of *voltigeurs* and fifty cavalry troopers, forthwith attacked across the bridge in a rush, broke the chains, overthrew the carts into the water, and moved onwards taking the village by storm. The cavalry followed on cutting down a number of peasants in their path. Torquemada was sacked and burned with few, if any, displays of mercy given to those discovered under arms.

It has been well noted that it is typical of soldiers to run rampant when faced with bands of irregulars not in uniform and there appears to be little doubt that the brutality of the fighting spilled over into non-combatants. Nevertheless, horrors were perpetrated at Torquemada which reflected the tone of the conflict that was to come. It has been suggested that his troops were running riot beyond Lasalle's control and that he did not approve of the extremities of brutality displayed by the French at Torquemada. However, Lasalle was indisputably the officer in command and must shoulder the responsibility for what transpired there.

'By destroying this village,' commented General Foy soberly, 'the French deprived themselves of the precious resources for the rest of the war.' We can take from this comment that Foy had

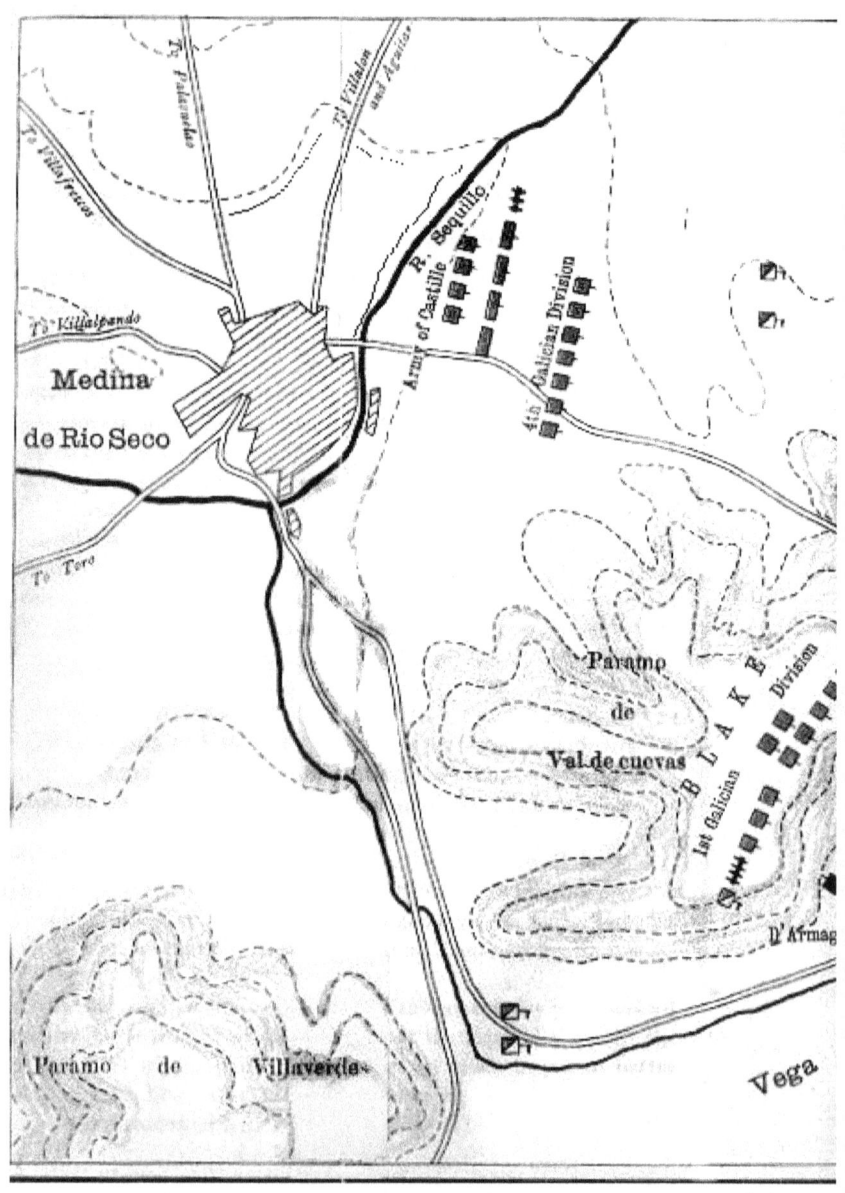

MAP OF

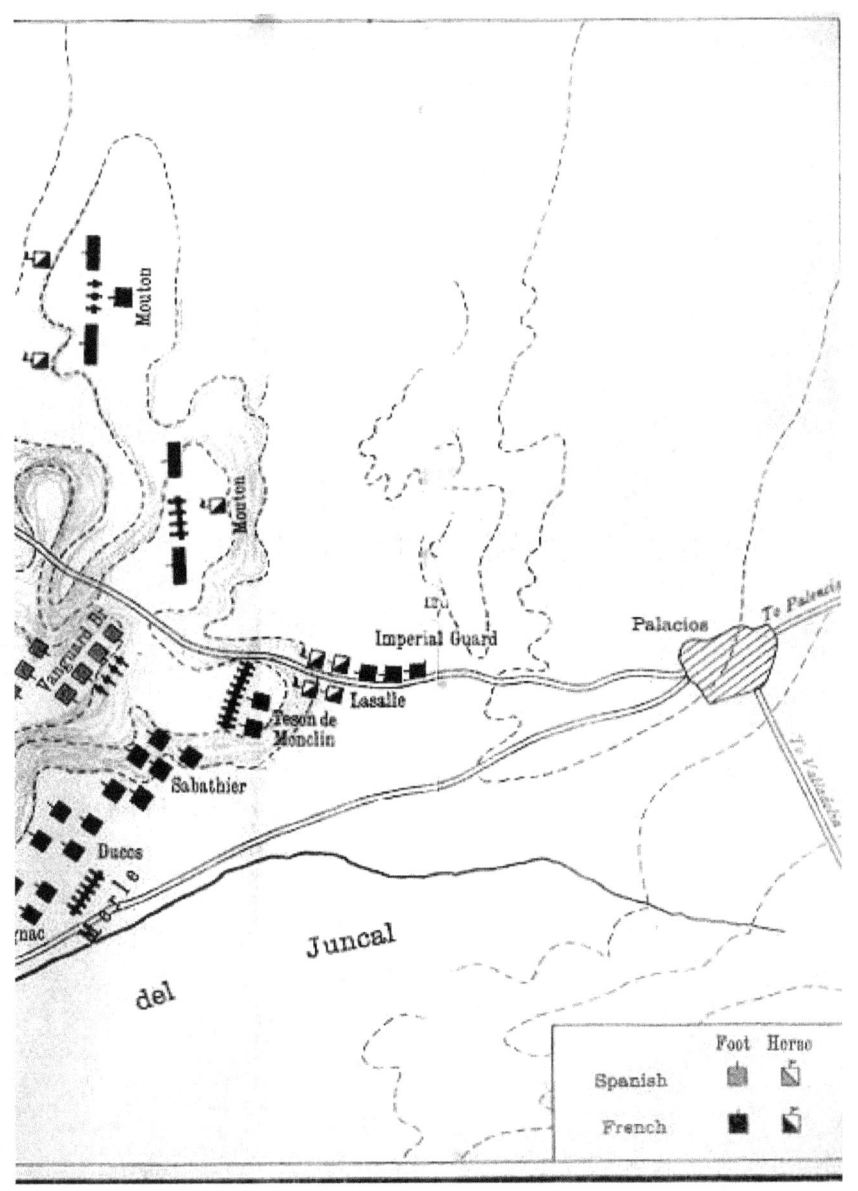

Medina de Rio Seco

in mind more far reaching consequences than might be materially found in a village in Spain. A far greater consideration was the resource of the compliance, cooperation and trust of the people of the countryside. If that was asking or expecting too much of an occupied people then placidity and acquiescence were no alternatives to be despised.

Foy implies that overt oppression gives certain being to uncompromising resistance and in this assertion, we cannot find him at fault. Whether it is entirely reasonable to lay the blame for this situation in the Peninsular War at Lasalle's feet on the basis of the one example of Torquemada is another matter. Lasalle's action in respect of the Spanish was not an incident in isolation, nor were his actions the first or last of their kind perpetrated by the French Army during this terrible war.

It is probably reasonable to suggest that Lasalle was largely unrepentant about his behaviour at Torquemada and there is little point in measuring him by the standards of modern codes of conduct in warfare whether those, indeed, are uniformly followed or not in reality. At the beginning of this war Lasalle had apparently, according to Thoumas, formed the opinion (though we do not know why that is so, especially in consideration of Murat's responses to civilian opposition in Madrid) that the Spaniards were treated by French authorities 'with too much indulgence'. He was of the opinion that it was necessary to 'reduce them by terror', and that in every conquered part of the country where a Frenchman was killed, a Spaniard had to be hanged in reprisal and that wherever there was an insurrection it was necessary to hang Spanish examples in quantity. Given what we now know of the practices of the French Army in Spain during this period, it is impossible to ameliorate their conduct as it applied to the population at large and that must, therefore, embrace Lasalle's activities for he was no exception to the rule.

The sacking and the burning of Torquemada had, indeed, carried terror into the country; the 3,000 or 4,000 Spaniards who guarded the city of Placencia, some 22 kilometres distant fled at the news and the approach of the French columns. Accordingly, the town found itself left to its own devices. The Bishop of Placencia came out to meet Lasalle with a deputation and asked with some understandable trepidation for mercy on behalf of his city.

Since it was known that the local clergy had conducted themselves well on the whole by rescuing several officers and soldiers of the French Army from the fury of the local inhabitants inflamed by notions of vengeance, Lasalle was inclined to be sympathetic or, at least, cooperative on this occasion. As a precaution, however, he ordered that all the inhabitants of the township to be disarmed, and, in concert with the bishop, took the 'necessary measures to secure the tranquillity of the countryside'. What that entailed exactly we may imagine.

Merle's division eventually joined him at Placencia and the force marched onwards towards Valladolid, which had risen in full insurrection. A Spanish corps, commanded by Don Gregorio de Cuesta, with a force of 7,000 men, of whom about a thousand were regular soldiers together with a few hundred *élite* cavaliers (the Queen's bodyguards and *Gendarmes*) were posted at the Cabezon bridge barring the way. Lasalle attacked the Spaniards with his usual resolution and his cavalry overthrew Don Cuesta's mounted troops. The French infantry likewise drove the Spanish bands back, the bridge was crossed, and the fugitives were killed in numbers as they ran. (Foy, *Histoire de la guerre de la Péninsule*, t. II.)

Lasalle, entering Valladolid, once again consented at the bishop's request, to pardon the town. He installed his headquarters there, and, in charge of the administration of the province, soon acquired, by his efficient management, popularity in Spain among the chiefs of the French Army. He apparently did not exacerbate his unpopularity with the local population by adding a further levy for his own requirements to the taxes levied upon them by the government. Perhaps surprisingly given what we mostly know of his character, Lasalle was apparently capable of displaying some diplomacy when the need arose. Consequently, he was considered to be frank and persuasive in his dealing with the Spanish people. He was able, moreover, to lean skilfully on the clergy to elicit their assistance to achieve his objectives, which was invaluable to him since the church was so politically influential.

Nevertheless, there can be little doubt of the difficulties and perils that came the way of Lasalle and his men whilst stationed in Spanish towns or indeed if travelling in the countryside alone or in small numbers. The officer of *cuirassiers*, Aymard Olivier Le Harivel de Gonneville was campaigning in this part of Spain at this period and so shared Lasalle's experience. He reported 'hateful countenances all round' in the streets of towns and villages. Assassination was common and increasing until 'it was not safe to leave the assemblage of the troops.' Hippolyte Piré so annoyed Napoleon at Somo-Sierra later in the campaign (by telling him the unvarnished, but unpalatable truth, concerning the feasibility of a proposed attack) that the emperor struck at him with his whip. This fall from favour soon thereafter resulted in Piré being dispatched alone on a mission around Madrid, which was considered by Gonneville at the time to be so perilous as to amount to a virtual death sentence, though, as it transpired, it was not.

Irrespective of how well Lasalle conducted his administrative affairs in Spain it is implausible, given he was an officer of an occupying army that had a record of ruthless and brutal subjugation, in which he had taken part himself a very few miles from his present headquarters, that the population at large did not fear and roundly hate him and all he represented.

To emphasise the point Gonneville wrote of this period:

> This war had now assumed a character of reciprocal animosity, which took its origin from the events that happened in Madrid in the month of May; animosity that kept on increasing and was a presage of atrocities quite beyond any before committed. These presages were realised, and the traditional tortures of the Inquisition were often put upon the wretched Frenchmen who fell into the hands of their pitiless adversaries; they were crucified

and sawn in two between planks. We saw a dragoon officer nailed against a door, having between his teeth the proof of the previous mutilation he had been subjected to. On the road we found a civilian *cantinière* (woman seller of goods) and a child of twelve with their throats cut; they were artistically disposed to display the barbarity that accompanied the act, and similar examples were repeated every moment.

In the meantime, the army corps under Marshal Bessières had been reorganised on new bases. It included the two divisions of Mouton's and Merle's infantry, the first of which was composed of old experienced French regiments. Lasalle took command of the cavalry, comprised of the 10th, 22nd and 26th Chasseurs à Cheval and a provisional regiment of dragoons.

The Spanish generals Joaquín Blake y Joyes (whose father was an Irishman) and Don Gregorio de Cuesta had combined their forces upon a gently sloped position at Medina de Río-Seco, on the frontier of Galicia. Cuesta had overall command. Despite recent setbacks, the Spanish generals were determined to continue their resistance and by taking up their position go some way in disrupting lines of communication between Madrid and France. On June the 13th Lasalle's scouts discovered the Spanish force which, although not fully consolidated at that point, was substantial and considerably outnumbered the approaching French.

In a display of poor military management, the Spanish generals not only positioned their forces on poor defensive ground but split their forces in half. In fact, the gap between the Spanish forces was approaching a mile wide which was a fatal error to make before a marshal of France.

Marshal Bessières, attacked them on the 14th of July by pinning down Cuesta with a smaller holding action whilst outflanking Blake with the mass of his infantry. After an hour Lasalle was let loose in the widening gap where they assaulted Blake's unprotected left flank. Lasalle's cavalry, supported by 300 *chasseurs* and Grenadiers à Cheval of the Imperial Guard succeeded, by repeated charges, in breaking the Spanish lines and Blake's defence crumpled and, with the notable exception of a square of Navarre infantry, quit the field in retreat. Cuesta put up a solid resistance for a while longer, including a counter attack, but his position was untenable and he ordered a retreat. Lasalle's cavalry thereafter galloped onwards to harry the enemy fugitives as they fled.

The pursuit continued for several days and was prosecuted with the utmost vigour, but some military commentators on the affair hold that if Bessières had marched on rapidly in the footsteps of his cavalry with the bulk of his force, he might have obtained even more decisive results which would have significantly influenced the campaign generally.

General Foy, who fought in Spain and wrote extensively on the conflict, in examining the particulars of the event suggests, for example, that it would have been very easy for Bessières to have communicated with Junot to ensure concerted action which would have assured the retreat of the Army of Portugal through Galicia. Foy went so far as to express his regret that the activity and ardour of Lasalle was in a broader sense wasted, chained as it was by the formal orders of Bessières, which forbade him to prosecute the pursuit to the fullest.

The point is a valid one, though there was little to guarantee the cooperation at this time of one French commander with another solely because he was asked to do so, irrespective of whether the tactic was sound or not. Junot's army, it must be noted, was in poor condition, even though it had faced virtually no opposition. Nor indeed has it ever been uncommon that a general did not follow up a battlefield victory with the action required to bring about a definitive conclusion. Lost opportunities have ever been commonplace on battlefields, just as the benefit of hindsight has always been a thing of wonder.

Nevertheless, the Battle of Medina de Río-Seco had filled Napoleon with joy for he felt that it demonstrated that Spain itself had now been conquered. 'It is the new Villaviciosa!' the emperor exclaimed triumphantly.

This remark was an allusion to the victory won in the battle of that name in 1710 during the War of Spanish Succession when a Franco-Spanish Army under the joint commands of Louis-Joseph, Duke of Vendôme and Philip V of Spain beat a Habsburg-Allied Army under Starhemberg in Guadalajara, Spain. Both sides claimed a victory at the time, but the strategic consequences of the action were that it had secured to the grandson of Louis XIV the crown of Spain. Napoleon, apparently believed that the victory at Medina de Rio-Seco presaged the same kind of outcome for the House of Bonaparte.

Unfortunately, and not for the first or last time. Napoleon's enthusiasm had pre-empted the outcomes of developing events and he was soon to be disabused of his opinions and aspirations regarding the straightforward usurping of the Spanish throne. The French were certainly right to believe that the Spanish Army alone might be ultimately no match for them, but that perspective was far from a situation in which the enemy army was on the brink of defeat with no will to fight left to it, as he was very soon to discover.

Just five days after the battle fought at Medina de Rio-Seco, the Battle of Baylen, (Bailén), was fought on July 19th, 1808 in Jaen province in the south of Spain. It brought about the first open field defeat of a Napoleonic army in any of its conflicts and there can be little doubt that had the emperor ever countenanced such an eventuality it would not have been brought about in his imaginings by a Spanish Army. General Foy was, one may suppose, less surprised since he had concluded that the Spanish army's performance at Medina de Rio-Seco was far better than anyone might have legitimately expected. The French general who suffered the ignominy of this defeat was General Pierre Dupont de l'Étang who, readers will recall, was the unfortunate object of the duelling obsession of Lasalle's truculent friend, François Fournier.

Dupont compounded this defeat (which came about as a result of his own poor judgement by not quitting Andalusia in the first place and secondly by allowing himself to be all but surrounded) by calling upon the Spanish for an armistice which resulted in his surrendering 18,000 French troops into captivity. News of the catastrophe at Baylen arrived in Madrid and shook French confidence, which negated the advantages that had been gained by Bessières in the north. A rattled King Joseph abandoned Madrid, rallied the corps of Moncey and Bessières, and retired to Miranda on the River Ebro. Lasalle, with his division, formed the rear-guard in this retreat, and, by manoeuvring, managed to keep the Spaniards at a comparatively safe distance.

Nevertheless, this reversal encouraged Spanish insurgents to rise up and become active all over the country. Further abroad the realisation that French armies were not after all invincible inspired nations which had fought them, suffered defeat and lapsed into despair to return to the struggle against Napoleon and this, following the clarion calls of a revitalised Austria, went some way to lead to the outbreak of the War of the Fifth Coalition.

Dupont was, of course, disgraced by Napoleon and recalled to France where he was sent for court martial, stripped of his rank and title and for a time imprisoned. Understandably, Dupont did not join Napoleon during The Hundred Days and in consequence prospered under the restoration of the Bourbons. Dupont appears to have been a man fated to be swept up by extremes of bad and good fortune. Perhaps his greatest good fortune was that he was not an Ottoman general whose failings of this magnitude would have resulted in execution by the bowstring. Indeed, lesser transgressions during the French revolutionary period in the very recent past had sent senior officers to the guillotine.

★★★★★★★★★★★

The army corps of Marshal Bessières, taking over the general organisation of the 2nd Army of Spain, proceeded under the orders of Marshal Soult, who came to take command of the army in Miranda and there it remained in enforced inaction until the arrival of the Emperor. It was evident to Napoleon that matters had become seriously unravelled in Spain and he, quite correctly, decided that it would require his own intercession to pull them back on course.

In November, Bessières was ordered to march on the city of Burgos, which was occupied by the Spanish troops of the province of Extremadura. In the combats which ensued as the consequence of this order, the French infantry took the leading part, for the fighting consisted of actions over rough terrain, of manoeuvring through wooded areas and assaulting heights.

The Battle of Burgos (also called Gamonal) was fought on November 10th, 1808. Once the infantry had achieved its objectives and the Spanish under Belveder began to retreat, Lasalle and Milhaud, who commanded a division of dragoons, pressed forwards in pursuit of the vanquished army, leaving it no respite, and slaughtering the fugitives as they retired. Credit must be given to the Spanish on this occasion for this was no orderless rout. Walloon Guards under Quesada formed a dogged rearguard and stood against Lasalle's repeated charges. Of the 307 men of this rear-guard just 74 of them survived. Among them was the wounded Quesada whose sword, it is reported, was returned to him by Bessières in honour of the heroism of his men.

No French general of cavalry of his time was more brilliant than Lasalle and it is inarguable that, as a light cavalry officer few knew their business better in pursuit. Bessières on this occasion was not in a position to hold Lasalle back and Napoleon, on the contrary, sent him all the way to the foot of the heights of Guadarrama. His division was no longer part of the 2nd corps but was attached to the general reserve of cavalry. The way was now open to central Spain and with that, of course, the main prize of the capital, Madrid, was ripe for the retaking.

The Battle of Somo-Sierra was fought on November 30th, 1808 some 60 miles north of Madrid. The French Army was under the command of the emperor himself and the heavily outnumbered Spanish force under Benito de San Juan was positioned to block the passage to the capital in the Guadarrama Pass, near Segovia. Napoleon launched an attack of combined arms which became notable for the decisive charge of the Polish light cavalry which, it is said, surged through its objectives to the battle cry of, 'Forward, you sons of dogs—the Emperor is watching' in Polish. Madrid fell within a matter of days. San Juan's men displayed their dissatisfaction with his leadership abilities by assassinating him.

Lassalle resumed his course southwards, and without stopping at Madrid pushed onwards through nearby Aranjuez and Toledo to Talavera and drove out the Spanish bands, which occupied the bridge of Almaraz on the Tagus.

17. Lasalle in Spain, 1809

In March, 1809, Lasalle, with his division, composed, according to Thoumas, of the 5th and 10th Chasseurs à Cheval, the Polish Lancers and the 2nd Hussars, was under the command of Marshal Victor. Other references cite the above regiments, but with the 9th Dragoons present instead of the Poles. Spanish insurgents had taken over the bridge of Almaraz in Extremadura in the province of Cáceres and destroyed it. Victor having been ordered to march on Andalusia, Lasalle formed his vanguard, and crossed the Tagus on another bridge at Arzobispo. The flank of the Spanish Army of Extremadura under Cuesta was thus turned, the bridge of Almaraz was then restored, and Victor marched towards the Guadiana.

Lasalle's cavalry (specifically the 5th Chasseurs à Cheval) had an engagement, on March 20th (Thoumas says 21st), at Trujillo with the Spanish Royal Carabiniers. The present writer has elected to abide with Thoumas in the name of this engagement since it appears to be located, as one would expect as regards the campaign leading to Medellin, though other references cite Berrocal as the location. All expected a battle to be fought the following day, but the Spanish Army decamped during the night. Lasalle rushed to follow on in its tracks. He had with him some infantry in the form of four companies of light infantry (voltigeurs), who took the lead position in the column when the vanguard had to cross country hindered by hills and woodlands, which was impractical for cavalry.

Once in the plain however, the 10th Chasseurs à Cheval,

commanded by Colonel Subervie, resumed the head of the column, pressing closely upon the enemy's rear-guard and slashing at it whenever the opportunity arose. This rear-guard under Henestrosa eventually withdrew to rejoin the main body of the Spanish Army. Subervie allowed himself to be dragged away from the support of the main body of Lasalle's cavalry and his *chasseurs* were separated from the column for more than an hour before concerns began to be raised as to their whereabouts. In fact, the Spaniards had drawn Subervie into an area beneath wooded hills and there, on the road near the village of Miajadas, 23 miles from Trujillo, lay in ambush. Many squadrons of their best cavalry (the Almanza and Infante regiments have been cited) had there been adroitly concealed and these fell upon the scattered and disordered *chasseurs*. Chaos ensued as the French horses were too tired from their recent exertions to rally and form.

The bloody business took but a few minutes and at least one hundred or more *chasseurs* were quickly *hors de combat*. Some sixty of the Frenchmen were taken prisoner, according to Thoumas, but were promptly massacred by the Spanish in the most cruel manner and their bodies odiously mutilated. The surviving *chasseurs* extricated themselves with great difficulty and rode for their lives. This was, alas, another shameful episode in a war which abounded with incidents of a brutality fostered by genuine hatred.

Lasalle, when he was informed of what was going on, set off at full speed to assist the *chasseurs* at the head of the 2nd Hussars, but the enemy's cavalry, satisfied with the *coup de main*, had, by the time he arrived at the scene of carnage, galloped away to rejoin the main body of the Spanish Army. Lasalle and his *hussars* swore to avenge this atrocity to their comrades and, as it transpired, their opportunity to do so came just a few days afterwards.

★★★★★★

Jacques-Gervais Subervie survived the catastrophe that befell his men in Spain and continued to serve throughout the wars of the empire including the disastrous Russian Campaign which he also survived. Thoumas, it must be noted in respect of his performance during the disaster in Spain, comments that he 'did not survive by a great display of courage', which rather implies the historian believed or possessed some evidence that Subervie had abandoned his men to their fate. Some two hundred years after the fact, one can only report that there is no hint of censure in Subervie's record following this incident. One can find no mention of, for example, an 'affair of honour' following this matter, which could be readily provoked by circumstances less extreme. Furthermore, his record before and after the event reveals him to be a very active soldier given to the displays of courage one might expect of a light cavalry officer of Napoleon's army. He rallied to Napoleon for the Campaign of 1815 where he commanded the 5th cavalry division within Pajol's I Cavalry Corps comprising the 1st and 2nd Lancers, the 11th Chasseurs à Cheval and two batteries of horse artillery. Together with Marbot's hussars it was these light cavalrymen who attempted to stem the advancing tide of the Prussian army as it debouched from woodland and onto the field of Waterloo.

★★★★★★

Lasalle's next combat came in the Battle of Medellin, fought on March 28, 1809, and it has remained as one of Lasalle's most notable battlefield claims to fame. It is also one of the most striking and decisive victories won by the French at this stage of the conflict against the Spanish. A comparatively small army of 12,000 to 15,000 Frenchmen under Victor defeated about 30,000 Spaniards under Gregorio de la Cuesta on the field of battle. The killed or wounded of the defeated enemy was numbered at more than 10,000 men and additionally, an enormous number of prisoners were taken; estimated in Marshal Jourdan's report at some 12,000. This battle marked the first major inroad into southern Spain following the debacle of Baylen, leading to the all but decisive Battle of Ocaña later in the year.

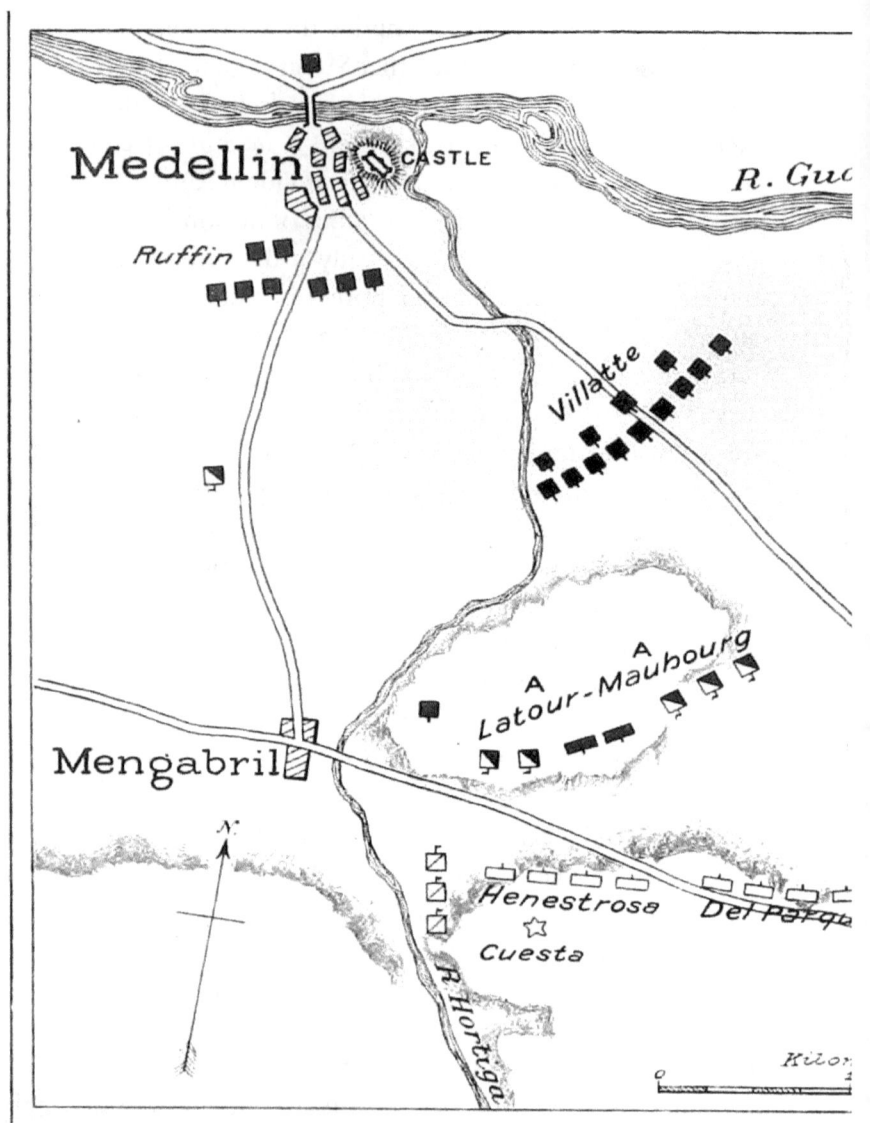

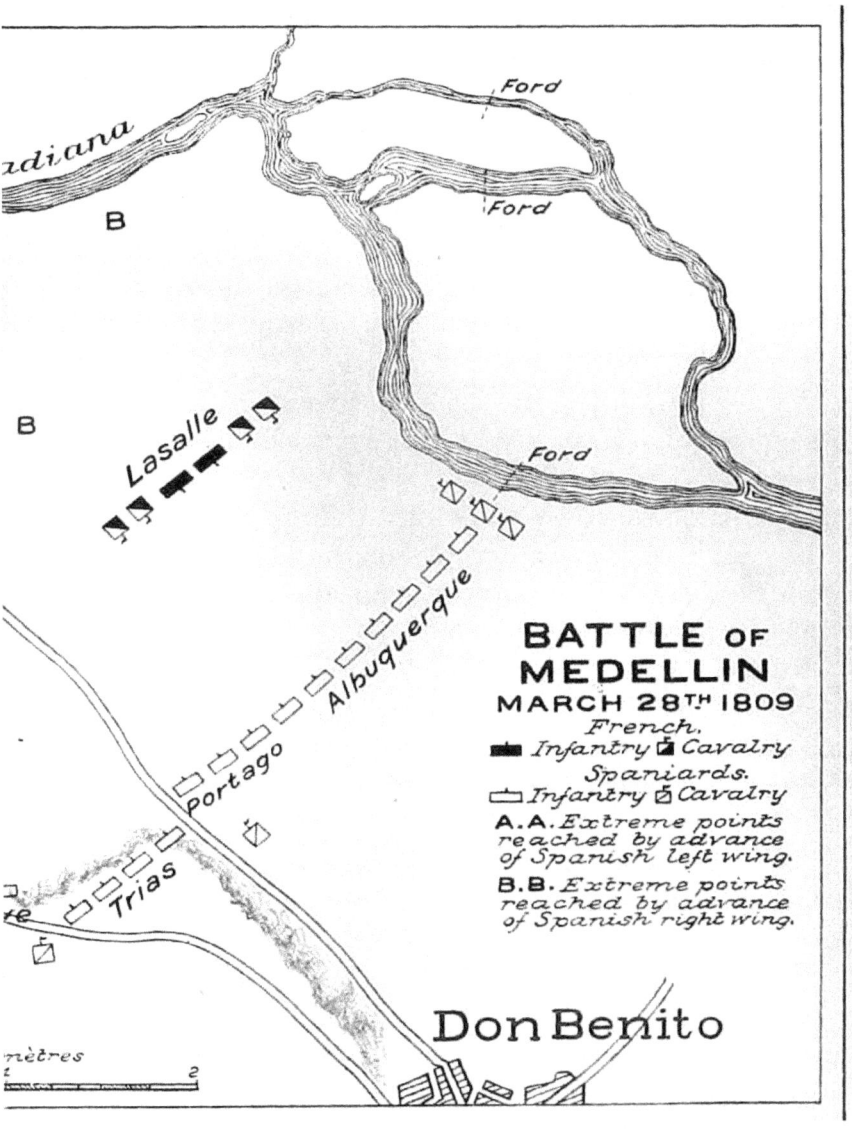

★★★★★★

Adolphe Thiers, in his writings reduces this Spanish figure to 4000 men killed or wounded but this is considered a conservative estimate.

★★★★★★

In this battle, cavalry and horse artillery played a leading role. Marshal Víctor had placed on his right La Tour-Maubourg's division of dragoons, and on his left Lasalle's cavalry division, supported by 2,000 infantry. The horse artillery opened a significant gap in the Spanish infantry lines, through which the dragoons charged, which ensured the left of the enemy's army was put to a complete rout, whereupon it was pursued at length by La Tour-Maubourg's horsemen and the German infantry of the Confederation of the Rhine under Leval.

Meanwhile, Lasalle, with his 2,000 horses and 2,500 infantrymen, was almost crushed by the centre and the right of the Spaniards. Forced to fall back so as not to be surrounded and to be caught in a bend in the River Guadiana, which was close at his rear, Lasalle retreated stubbornly, turning to impede the Spaniards by charges when their advance became bold to the point of potentially successful enterprise.

Lastly, the enemy's cavalry having prepared to attack a squadron of the 2nd Hussars, which formed the extreme rear-guard, was nonplussed when this squadron turned round and waited for them with, according to Thoumas, 'such haughty and calm countenance' that the Spanish lancers, apparently discouraged by this calmness, advanced hesitantly, and the *commandant* of the *hussars* took advantage of it to throw his men upon theses lancers, and went on to also overthrow the squadrons which followed behind them. Thoumas' version possibly errs on the romantic in its interpretation of events, but it is beyond doubt that the French cavalry delivered the *coup de grace* at Medellin.

Lasalle, whose talent was that he never lost sight of any of the influential movements of the field of battle, saw an opportunity for a decisive counter attack, signalled to all his division which, turning and forming in line at 'a great trot', swept away everything before it. At the same moment a battery of horse artillery, from the right to the left of the French Army, came to shoot at the right wing of the Spaniards. In a few moments, this wing was put in a complete rout; the soldiers threw away their arms to escape more quickly.

Latour-Maubourg's cavalry, on returning from pursuing the left wing, barred the passage to the fugitives. Thoumas informs us that the French cavalry at this point ran out of hand which he explains thus:

> Our cavaliers were irritated by the long resistance of the enemy, furious to meet among the ranks of the troops of the peasants without uniform, to which they attributed the ferocious massacre of the enemy, sixty cavalry of the 10th Chasseurs à Cheval and they began to sabre the vanquished, making no quarter.

This was to be Lasalle's final Spanish battle and it ended in ignominy for the French embarked on a retaliatory killing spree, which included quantities of prisoners.

Quantities of Spanish guns and colours fell into the hands of Marshal Victor's army. The jubilant French commander compiled a glowing report of the action and foremost among the names of generals who received praise for their actions during the Medellin campaign was that of Lasalle.

On the eve of the battle, that is to say, on March 27, 1809, the Emperor had signed Lasalle's appointment to the command of the 1st Light Cavalry Division of the army which was to campaign in Germany.

18. Lasalle Leaves Spain, 1809

Hostilities had already begun on the Danube when Lasalle's letter of nomination reached its recipient in Spain, who was with his command on the banks of the Guadiana. Lasalle was elated with his latest appointment and hurried to ready himself for departure. There was not a moment to lose if he wished to arrive in time to fully take part in the war in which Napoleon was to lead the army personally. To fight under the eyes of the Emperor was then the ideal for all the officers and generals of the empire. Lasalle closed his affairs and military duties, hurriedly packed his belongings and left immediately on his journey, accompanied only by an *aide-de-camp*.

Thiébault appears to have recorded a part of this event with delightful graphic detail in his memoirs.

> It was half past three in the morning and I was fast asleep, when I was roused with a start by the creaking of my door as it was thrown suddenly open, by the disorderly noise of boots, spurs, a scrape of a trailing sabre and by hearing a voice shouting loud enough to split my head.
>
> "I am thirsty, I am hungry", it announced. It was that amiable lunatic Lasalle who had galloped in advance of his equipages to pass the day with me accompanied only by his *aide-de-camp*, Du Coëtlosquet, who in those days acted as joker and humorist to people whose assassin he was one day to become.

★★★★★★

Thiébault has made a harsh comment about Du Coëtlosquet here because he felt very strongly about those men who had served the empire and prospered from it, but who then embroiled themselves in the reprisals against former comrades under the Restoration of the Bourbons. Charles Yves César du Coëtlosquet joined the army in 1800 as a soldier in the 10th Hussars and remained the consummate cavalryman.

By 1802 he had become an officer and *aide-de camp* to General Millet. He became Lasalle's *aide-de-camp* in January, 1806 and was with him at Wagram. By 1812 he was the colonel of the 8th Regiment of Hussars. Promoted brigadier-general in 1813, he commanded a brigade of light cavalry at the Battle of Montereau, February 13th, 1814. This battle, fought south-east of Paris, was one within the final brilliant campaign which Napoleon directed as emperor. As it transpired Montereau, which was a French victory, was notable for the exceptional contribution of the cavalry.

After Napoleon's flight from Elba, Du Coëtlosquet not only did not rally to his former master's banner, but commanded Royalist forces which opposed him. He prospered during the Bourbon Restoration rising to the rank of lieutenant-general and subsequently served as Minister of War in 1823.

Despite Thiébault's judgement and without exploring the intricate details of his behaviour and activities during the Restoration period, Du Coëtlosquet unambiguously served the legitimate government of his nation all his days and he was not alone among former imperial officers in condemning men who had been erstwhile comrades. Lasalle's friend La Tour-Maubourg, it will be recalled, was one of them. Du Coëtlosquet died in Paris in 1836, aged just 52 years old.

★★★★★★

Thiébault fondly, remembered:

Before my servant had time to bring candles I had leapt

out of bed and embraced poor Lasalle, who was on his way to join the Grand Army. Interested in all that could interest me, he must needs visit my quarters, my hospitals, the fort—not like Suchet, for his own profit, but out of pure friendship for me. When he heard how I had got rid of Ballesteros, he congratulated me on the result which the course of events had given to the base conduct of Marshal Mortier, maintaining that if Mortier had left me a regiment no one would have thought of the deputation of which I had made use to correspond with Ballesteros; if I had had any troops, I should have thought only of defending myself, and, being too weak to hold out, I should have been done for. Thus, all was for the best in the best of worlds.

This anecdote serves to underline the genuine quality of loyalty that was an integral part of Lasalle's character. Lasalle could be relied upon to wholeheartedly support his friends and some of this conversation concerns an important incident in Thiébault's career. Readers interested in that subject in further detail are encouraged to investigate Thiébault's own extensive and interesting autobiography. However, in this context Thiébault's editor has issues with it.

This meeting took place on April 28th according to Thiébault's editor.

> Some days, therefore, before Ney and Kellermann entered the Asturias, and some weeks before Ballesteros had left that province and marched upon Santander; so that the rumour as to that general having been close to Burgos, previously to this must have been unfounded. In any case, Burgos would hardly have been on his way from Oviedo to Santander, though, knowing that the place was defenceless after its troops had been summoned to Kellermann, he may have detached a force to look at it. But this cannot have been till May, so that in any case Thiébault's recollections here must have got confused.

PIERRE-LOUIS RŒDERER,

COMTE DE L'EMPIRE,

Sénateur, Ministre-Secrétaire d'État du Grand-Duché de Berg,
Grand-Officier de la Légion d'Honneur.

'I'll arrive late in any event and be scolded for it,' Lasalle said to his friends during a convivial meal, referring to the reception he expected upon his arrival, by Napoleon 'So I shall not leave Paris until I have ordered a pair of boots.'—*Souvenir de Roederer*.

'That day gained me another visit—from M. Roederer, who was on his way from Paris to Madrid,' we are told by Thiébault in confirmation of this encounter, 'He dined with us, and the meal was remarkable for certain discussions upon high topics, in which Lasalle was magnificent."

'After the meal upon leaving the table, M. Roederer took me, (Thiébault), aside and said, "I was acquainted with General Lasalle as the most brilliant of our light cavalry generals; I knew that he was witty and valiant, but I was miles from crediting him with the high ability which distinguishes him. He is a man of surpassing talent; his mind and his learning are no less deep than brilliant."

'Nor was there anything exaggerated in this eulogy,' says Thiébault

Roederer took notes of the conversation, and his report of it will be found in the Appendix at the end of vol. viii. of Sainte-Beuve's *Causeries du Lundi*. Not much trace appears of the 'discussions *d'un ordre élevé*,' but as a picture of bright table-talk it is admirable.

Lasalle undoubtedly intended to be travelling at full speed towards France and did not accept, despite the dangers of the road, an escort of troopers that would have slowed down his course. Once again, Thiébault provides us with a personally observed insight of Lasalle as he disentangled himself from the impediment of his accompanying troops upon their parting.

'We had hardly left the dinner table' remembered Thiébault, 'than we must have punch, and that in great bowls in rapid sequence. Then the fun began, and Du Coëtlosquet's turn came. I do not know how many scenes he performed, or how many Bacchanalian verses he did not sing us, but he acquitted himself to the delight of all. Towards ten o'clock Lasalle's equipages arrived; he had given his orders, and post-horses were harnessed to his carriage. After the most affectionate embraces and wishes which Heaven was never to grant, as he had his foot on the step he declared, "What's all that?" noticing for the first time five mounted *chasseurs* of the Nassau Regiment waiting nearby.

"It is an escort, which will accompany you as far as Celada," replied Thiébault

"I told you I wouldn't have an escort," retorted Lasalle. There had, indeed been some dispute on the subject of escorts between the friends during dinner.

"And I choose that you shall be escorted," insisted Thiébault, who was obviously justifiably concerned for Lasalle's safety.

"*Donnerwetter!*" exclaimed Lasalle addressing the *chasseurs* in German, "If you attempt to escort me I will jump on the postillion's horse and charge you!"

******

A postillion is a person who rides upon the leading near-side horse of a team or pair drawing a coach or carriage. These riders were particularly employed in cases where there was no actual coachman. It is difficult to understand why anyone travelling virtually alone by coach through a hostile country known to be alive with guerillas, whose chosen prey was precisely the unguarded traveller that Lasalle here personified would chose, in their rational mind, to eschew the services of a mounted military escort.

Furthermore, we are told that the escort consisted of Nassau *chasseurs*. These German troops in French service were known to be of the highest calibre and, coincidentally, Thiébault himself, who knew them by close association, praised them so highly that he is on record as asserting that the Nassauian troops were unsurpassed in Spain. Unlikely though it is that Lasalle would have actually charged his intended escort, it may be that had he actually made the attempt he may well have discovered that he had 'his hands full' in dealing with them. By no measure could the Nassauian troopers be an impediment in any way to Lasalle travelling in a coach, for they were fine cavalrymen and we may assume they might have taken some justifiable offence at their rejection on this occasion.

So ultimately, we must attribute Lasalle's refusal to be escorted to simple obstinacy on his part.

On the 10th of December, 1813 as it became clear that the First Empire of the French was in its death throes, the Nassau troops left the French, having fought with distinction in over 40 battles, and marched over to the Allies to whom they then pledged their allegiance. At Waterloo in 1815, before the action the Duke of Wellington approached the Nassauian general, August von Kruse, and commented,' I hope, General, that your actions today are as clever when you are fighting for me as they were in Spain when you fought against me'.

★★★★★★

Thiébault concludes remorsefully:

> Thus we parted and he left me, rejoicing in the idea of adding to that harvest of laurels which he had already gathered on so many glorious battlefields. Exalted by his good luck, he was actually hastening to a death no less premature than deplorable. That day was, indeed, the last of his existence for me.

The friendly dispute between Thiébault and Lasalle on the question of the escort is also duly recorded by Monsieur Roederer in his writings.

The war in the Iberian Peninsula in 1809 had several years of bloodshed before it ere Wellington drove the armies of France back over the Pyrenees. In open battle the French Army could usually be relied upon to acquit itself capably against a similar Spanish force, but as has been emphasised earlier in this text, that remained far from the issue for small detachments of French

Nassau troops, Spain, 1810

troops at large in a hostile land where practically every Spaniard who could not be described as a collaborator was by degrees an enemy.

In a war to the knife, Spanish guerillas who knew the wild and sparsely populated terrain, were masters of the ambush and could melt invisibly into the population if necessary, were at a distinct advantage. Few roads in an occupied country are entirely safe for an invader to travel upon. Perhaps predictably these facts meant very little to a man like Lasalle who had decided he had somewhere to be in a hurry.

Nevertheless, upon one road to the north Lasalle arrived at a stretch which was well known to be preyed upon by guerilla bands. A French outpost was positioned to police the area and a road block impeded Lasalle's progress. Naturally he ordered it removed without delay, but the soldiers manning it, understandably nonplussed by the behaviour of this irate traveller who demonstrably out ranked them, called for their superior officer to resolve the problem.

The commander of the post approached Lasalle's carriage: 'General,' he said, for so much of this newcomer's status was obvious, 'I cannot let you go on without an escort of twenty-five men to accompany you. Brigands are known to be actively operating along your route.'

Lasalle once again refused the offer of an escort, and losing his temper as the *commandant* continued to insist that he should accept one, finally exclaimed, 'Do you know to whom you speak?'

'I speak to a French officer,' replied the post commander, which rather, though not unreasonably, suggests Lasalle was not attired at the time in the unique manner which would have made the enquiry and its response redundant nor indeed as we have become accustomed to imagine him wearing.

'You speak to General Lasalle. How many of these brigands are there in this band?'

'About three hundred,' replied the post commander.

'What!' exclaimed Lasalle, 'Just 300! You have fifty men under your command and yet you leave the road unsafe. That is cowardly. I will account for your conduct and I do not want your escort.'

This is an interesting anecdote and there is no doubt that in times gone by, Lasalle's reaction on this occasion would have spoken only to his personal courage. How any arbiter would evaluate this kind of behaviour from a modern general crossing an area known to be controlled by insurgents, for example, may be left to the imagination. How the unescorted Lasalle would have dealt with an ambush by Spanish guerillas on this journey remains moot.

Nevertheless, despite his quite genuine if reckless bravery, Lasalle's progress was not immune from the effects of the hostility of the Spanish population. As he had passed through Torquemada, south-west of Burgos, which he had burned ten months previously, an angry crowd of the villagers gathered outside the house in which he was resting, and would have done him harm if it had dared to attack a senior French officer in daylight.

As he left the village to continue his journey an incident occurred which amused Lasalle and he was known to have recounted it afterwards. As his carriage paused at the village post-house, now rebuilt with 6,000 *francs*, which he had given to the postmaster after the burning of the village, the wife of this individual presented herself at his carriage and asked its passenger whether it was true that General Lasalle had been killed.

'Yes! He is dead,' replied Lasalle, whether mischievously or wisely, given his location we cannot now know though probably the former. At that moment the husband also came to his carriage at that time and recognised him. In this story the postmaster, in spite of Lasalle's 'refusals and his protestations', thereafter carried to his carriage, 'as a sign of gratitude', *ALL* the eggs and chickens of the post-house of Torquemada.

It may seem churlish to question the veracity of anecdotes such as this, which when recounted by Thoumas were clearly intended to demonstrate that despite some of his less than admirable traits, Lasalle had genuine fine qualities to the extent that he could be deservedly held in genuine affection by simple

Spanish people.

However, Torquemada was a village that had recently been savagely dealt with by Lasalle as an invader. Indeed, the inhabitants had, on this very occasion, demonstrated their hostility towards him. That the post-house had been rebuilt after its destruction is not in question, though the implication that this was generously paid for by Lasalle personally since he had some particular affection for post-houses as homes for Spanish post-masters is quite implausible. It should be remembered that at one point, Lasalle, in an official capacity, had been involved in administrating the area. Now Lasalle was *en route* to France upon a well-travelled road and upon these roads both post-houses and post-masters were essentially required to maintain effective and unimpeded communications, including for French Army personnel. One may reasonably suppose it was for this reason that the post-house of Torquemada, which Lasalle had not hesitated to destroy, was quickly reinstated.

Furthermore, it is improbable that the post-master and his wife were unaware of this consideration and so knew that any domiciliary advantages accruing to them were incidental. No doubt the Spanish post-master fulfilled his responsibilities as regarded the French begrudgingly, but under no illusion that in this he had no other choice guaranteed to perpetuate his well-being. In fact, given their own village had been recently destroyed, any finer feelings the post-master and his wife may have had felt for Lasalle, however completely unlikely that would have been, would be viewed in a very poor light by their countrymen in these violent times in Spain. Any demonstration of partiality would, following the absence of French troops to protect them, have probably prompted a death sentence on grounds of treacherous collaboration for both of them.

Is it plausible that, at their most generous this couple, living in a country hard pressed by the deprivations of war and occupation by an army well known for its excesses, which violently took what it wanted with no thought of restitution, would have willingly pressed 'out of gratitude' their entire stock of eggs and the all means they had to produce more eggs and supply themselves with meat on a passing Frenchman, who they knew was the same man who was responsible for the miseries of all of their friends and neighbours?

It is more likely, surely that Lasalle, true to form for the French at the time, simply took what he wanted or indeed that the post-master's wife upon hearing of the 'death' of General Lasalle displayed an emotion other than unambiguous regret when asking for confirmation.

The extraordinarily extravagant 'gift' of every chicken and egg they possessed has, in the real world, the hallmarks of a desperate peace offering hastily pressed by two very frightened, impoverished people in the hope of mitigating offence and avoiding potential further reprisals of the kind that they knew this man was capable. Lasalle, it seems, for all his protestations actually took all the chickens and eggs so the 'gift' may be said to have fulfilled its purpose. In those circumstances the outcome was one for which the post-master and his wife actually had cause to feel some 'gratitude.' Indeed, it is entirely possible that the post-master's gift furnished the menu for Lasalle's meal with Thiébault and Roederer.

This hypothesis is not intended to judge Lasalle harshly for the present writer has no new information regarding this anecdote. We may readily believe that if the post-master's wife had committed a gaff then Lasalle had it within him as a prankster to laugh it off. Lasalle can never have been a man other than one of his nation and times and it behoves us, perhaps, to consider that fact before we too readily embrace glamorous versions of him, of which there are many, which have garnered authenticity simply by virtue of their longevity.

Lasalle

19. The War of the Fifth Coalition

The fact that there was a fifth coalition of allies (and, indeed, would be a sixth) opposed to France in this period serves to illustrate what a protracted period of unresolved conflict the years of the French Revolution, Consulate and First Empire of the French were. The new orders of Europe were, by their nature, a dangerous anathema to the continent's established powers. From the outset the French were constantly attempting to expand the influence of their philosophies and boundaries of their interests and in this they were as constantly challenged by those who knew that was France to have its way it would ultimately mean the end of them. Beyond possibility of a lasting compromise the final outcome had to be the complete defeat of one side or the other. That accepted, it was strategically impossible, given the size of respective populations available for military service, the geography of the homelands of the protagonists and resources of the allies, that these wars would end in a way other than that which actually transpired.

The coalitions of allied powers, in their various configurations, simply would not give up the fight against a radicalised nation and their failures to prevail, which resulted in greater gains for France in the short term, only created further enmity and impetus for renewed conflict. It is the will to continue the fight combined with the resources to do so that ultimately confounds high risk strategies such as those employed by Napoleon. History has demonstrated (in millennia prior to the Napoleonic age and on several occasions since its demise) that grinding at-

THE AUSTRIAN ARCHDUKE CHARLES

trition will be the deciding factor in warfare irrespective of the genius of generals or courage of soldiers. That this outcome was assisted by the fundamentally flawed reality of the age of revolution at the turn of the 18th and 19th centuries was no small consideration.

The War of the Fifth Coalition was an example of this scenario. Austria in 1809 was smarting from the enormous concessions it had been forced to accept by Napoleon as a consequence of previous defeats on the battlefield during The War of the Fourth Coalition, but it was not in a position where it was under compulsion without alternatives of redress to tolerate them.

The Austrian Archduke Charles formed an army of 300,000 men with a reserve of a further 200,000 men. He proposed to fight this war on four fronts. The main army known as 'The Army of Germany' under his own command consisting of 200,000 men would operate in the valley of the River Danube. The Archduke John would command 'The Army of Italy' of 60,000 men which would, as the name suggests, invade Italy. Archduke Ferdinand with his 40,000 men of 'The Army of Galicia' would enter the Grand Duchy of Warsaw. Jellachich would rouse the Tyrol with his force of 20,000 troops. Austria's allies, Britain, Portugal and Spain would be engaged in the Iberian Peninsula.

Napoleon responded by creating an 'Army of Germany' of 270,000 men in six corps of whom 80,000 were not French troops but from allies including Bavarians, Würtembergers, Hessians, Badeners and Saxons under Lannes, Davout, Masséna, Lefebvre, Vandamme, Bernadotte and Bessières. Jerome was in Westphalia with an army corps, Prince Eugène was in Italy, Marmont was in Dalmatia and Poniatowski was in Poland.

In January 1809 only Davout with 60,000 men was in Germany at Würzberg. However, the grand plan essentially entailed a move by French armies *en masse* towards the Austrian capital, Vienna, including the turning of the Austrian armies in the Tyrol and Italy whilst Poniatowski simply held in place any potential influence on the outcome by forces under the command of Archduke Ferdinand.

The storming of Ratisbon

Since we are primarily concerned with the career of Lasalle, focus in the text will be henceforth confined to a sketch of the campaign along the Danube to the close of the Battle Wagram. Berthier, who as Imperial Chief of Staff, commanded in Napoleon's absence, moved Davout to Ratisbon (Regensburg), Masséna to Augsberg and Lefebvre to the line of the River Isar. The Austrians, in mid-April, believing their opportunity was to destroy the French piecemeal in their dislocated state, conceived a typically complex plan which they delayed to implement in a timely fashion.

The French emperor arrived in theatre in time to decisively rectify matters in his own army and confound his enemy by his military genius. On April 17th Napoleon was at Donauwörth and immediately ordered the concentration of his forces. So, began the so called 'Campaign of the Five Days', April 19th-23rd, 1809. Five combats ensued in the wooded terrain between the River Danube and the River Isar.

Davout was victorious at Tengen on April 19th. Napoleon attacked and was victorious at Abensberg on the 20th. The Austrians retreated to Landshut with the French in pursuit and on April 21st, Napoleon drove them over the River Isar. The day previously the Austrians had entered Ratisbon to secure their passage over the Danube and on the 22nd offered battle at Eckmühl but were forced back into Ratisbon, securing the city with a garrison. Napoleon took Ratisbon on April 23rd. The Austrians had lost 50,000 men over the five-day campaign and their lines of communication were not only destroyed but their capital was now uncovered.

Napoleon then moved along the right bank of the Danube towards Vienna driving the enemy before him. He crossed the River Inn and inflicted another decisive defeat upon the Austrians at Ebersberg on the Traun on May 3rd. Vienna fell into the hands of the French (for the second time) on May 13th. Archduke Charles selected for a passage Ebersdorf, four miles below Vienna where the Danube is divided by the great island of Lobau destroying bridges across the river behind him. The stage was set for one of the bloodiest engagements of the Napoleonic wars: The Battle of Aspern-Essling.

20. The Battle of Aspern-Essling, May 21st, 1809

Arriving on the banks of the Danube opposite the island of Lobau, Masséna began the construction of a pontoon bridge of boats and on the morning of May 19th crossed over to the island. To gain passage to the further bank some bridges were thrown across at the re-entrant bend, the extremities of which were guarded by the villages of Aspern and Essling.

Lasalle had fought, on the 28th of March, in Spain on the Guadiana. Just over six weeks later on the 18th of May he waited in readiness to cross the Danube to the island of Lobau with his division of light cavalry. It is said that at the end of his long journey across Europe, having arrived during the night at Vienna where his divisional staff received him, he had sent for bottles of Champagne, a supply of tobacco and women for his *aides-de-camp* and his staff.

Lasalle learned that his former regiment, the 10th Hussars, was stationed about ten leagues from Vienna and so leaving his officers to their pleasures he mounted his horse and in the middle of the night rode towards the camp of the hussars where he had the men awakened to shake their hands and drink a toast with them before returning to take up his command in earnest.

The division, which the emperor had reserved for Lasalle comprised six regiments of light cavalry. According to the official account of the campaign of 1809, Lasalle had under his orders for the passage of the Danube and the Battle of Essling, twelve regiments, namely: three foreign regiments, (Freystadt's brigade comprising the Baden Light Dragoons, the Hesse-Darmstadt and Württemberg Chevau-légers), the 8th Hussars, and the 3rd, 11th, 13th, 14th, 16th, 19th, 23rd and 24th Chasseurs. If this was really so, it was because the light cavalry of Masséna's corps, commanded by Marulaz, was added for the occasion to this division since the regiments under Marulaz's command are included in the above list.

Be that as it may, Lasalle crossed with his cavalry over to the island of Lobau, on the ill-fated great bridge of seventy boats. In the afternoon of May 20th, a bridge of fifteen pontoons having been thrown on the little arm of the Danube, between the island of Lobau and the bank was crossed first by Lasalle leading his cavalry. Some companies of infantrymen (*voltigeurs*) had previously been transported on boats to the hostile shore, were already occupying the outlet on the bank.

Two divisions of infantry followed the light cavalry, that of Molitor, who occupied the valley of Aspern and that of Boudet, who settled in the village of Essling. Between these two villages the Danube had an elbow projecting towards the right bank; the line from Essling to Aspern, forming the rope of this arc, was marked by a broad ditch behind which a wood stretched. Lasalle, with his 5,000 horsemen, passed through the wood, crossed the ditch at a gallop, and swept out into the Marchfeld plain before them, throwing squadrons in every direction where they fanned out to reconnoitre the terrain seeking to make contact with the Austrian Army.

The reports these reconnaissances brought back were contradictory as to the strength, disposition and location of the Austrian army. Attempts to come in closer contact with the main body of the enemy were foiled by an effective barrier of Austrian cavalry. Lasalle knew well the role of the light cavalry at this time concerned intelligence gathering and since he had no orders, which would permit his cavalry to engage in combat, he gave instructions that his squadrons should fall back slowly to the ground behind the ditch. Once in position his division set up its bivouacs for the night among the comparatively small French force

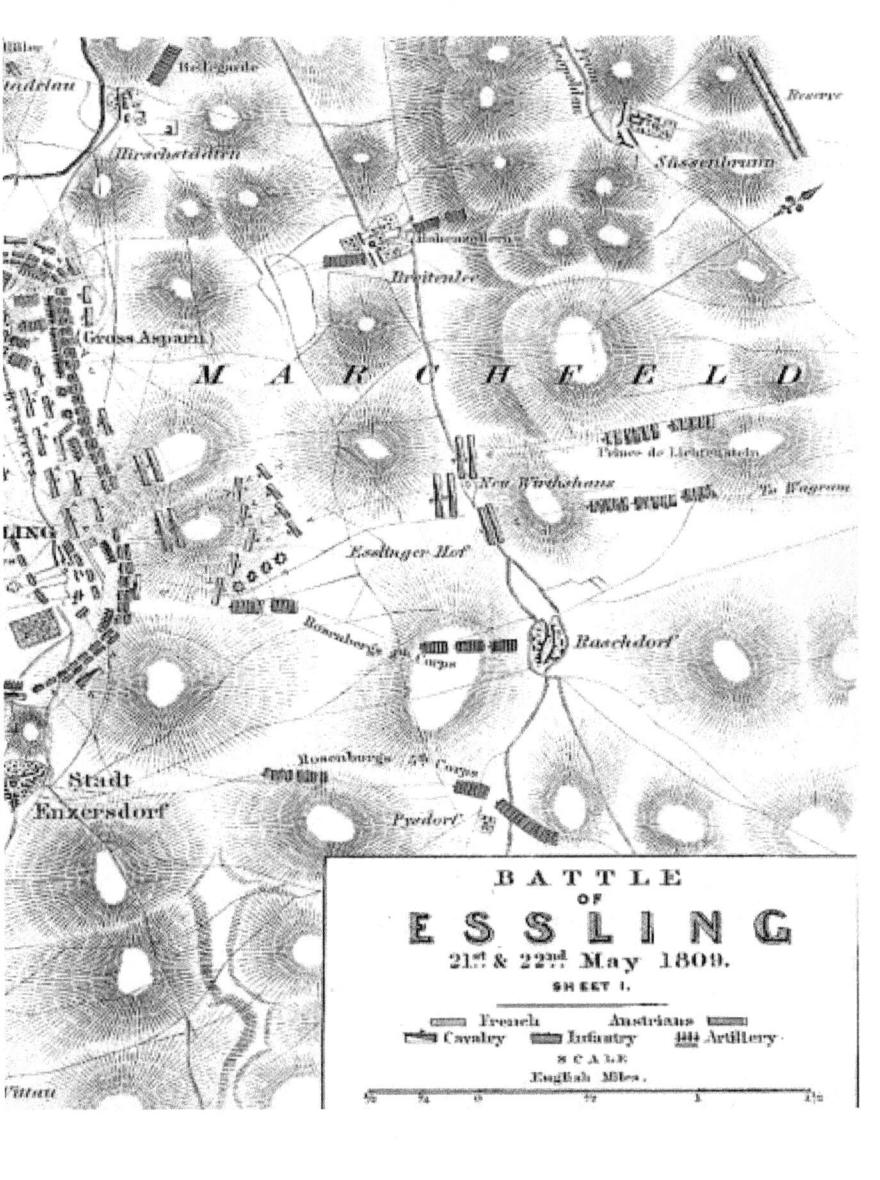

(now isolated by the breaking of the hastily constructed bridge of boats) that now occupied the hostile bank among which was now the person of the Emperor. Opposing them, invisible was an Austrian Army six times their present number.

At about midnight an unsettled Masséna was inspecting the lines occupied by the troops under his command. On arriving among the bivouacs of the light cavalry he discovered Lasalle who he woke from a deep untroubled sleep. Masséna was convinced that the enemy was at hand and said as much to Lasalle who reassured him, according to Pelet, saying that he was persuaded, based to the reports he had received of his reconnaissance, that the bulk of the Austrian Army was still far away. In this Lasalle was fundamentally and uncharacteristically mistaken. By this hour, however, there was no longer any doubt as to the proximity of the enemy army since in the darkness the lights of camp fires could now be seen among the Austrian bivouacs. How much of the Austrian main force this represented at this point no Frenchman in camp that night could with certainty know. (General Pelet, *Mémoires sur la guerre de 1809*).

On the morning, May 21st, there could be no doubt that the moment where battle would soon be joined was at hand. Fortunately, the bridge which enabled the balance of the French Army to cross the Danube had been repaired in the early hours and troops were moving steadily to join Napoleon. These reinforcements continued to arrive until 1 p.m. when, unfortunately, the bridge failed again. The French Army preparing for imminent battle had increased in numbers but remained outnumbered and stationary occupying an enclave in a place it had originally expected to simply pass through.

It was then that across the entire front in a great arc, the Austrian Army of some 100,000 men began to appear advancing from every point from west to east. Napoleon had less than 25,000 men under his immediate command for a defensive action where over 8,000 of them were cavalry though some of them were now Espagne's heavies—the *cuirassiers* who had arrived during the morning.

By 2.30 p.m. battle had been joined in earnest. At this point Lasalle was on the flank positioned behind Espagne's *cuirassiers* and the village of Essling in company with the cavalry commander, Bessières, and surrounded by his 8th Hussars, 16th Chasseurs, Württembergers and the 24th and 13th Chasseurs. Napoleon ordered his artillery to mass and defend his centre and sent Bessières with all his available cavalry into the attack on the advancing Austrian centre.

Espagne's *cuirassiers* broke through the Austrian cavalry dispersing them and onwards to the massed infantry, which formed square (or the Austrian version of it: the *battalionmasse*) to repel them. Repeated charges proved futile and whilst the *cuirassiers* were milling impotently around the Austrian infantry, the enemy's cavalry, which had not only rallied but had been reinforced, launched a counter attack, which sent the French cavalry flying for the protection of its own lines. As the *cuirassiers* cleared the field, French artillery batteries tore into the pursuing Austrian squadrons. The contest, however, remained hard fought with the village of Aspern in flames, being lost and retaken several times.

Around 5 p.m. the boat bridge once again became passable and more French troops began to cross over the Danube, including Saint Sulpice's and Nansouty's cavalry divisions. Every infantryman and horseman were by this point desperately needed, for casualties were in some units that had contested the fiercest assaults running up to fifty percent.

At 6 p.m. the French cavalry once more assailed the Austrian centre. Bessières ordered Espagne's, Saint Sulpice's and part of Nansouty's division to the charge and they went into action furiously. After the success of the initial inertia of the blow, this attack foundered as fresh Austrian cavalry once again counter attacked. The *cuirassiers* recoiled but were saved from destruction by the intercession of the light cavalry of Marulaz and Piré. Counter charge followed charge pointlessly for an hour or so. Cavalry of either side that overstepped their boundaries were savaged by infantry fusillade or cannister fire from artillery.

Thoumas has Lasalle involved at this time in company with

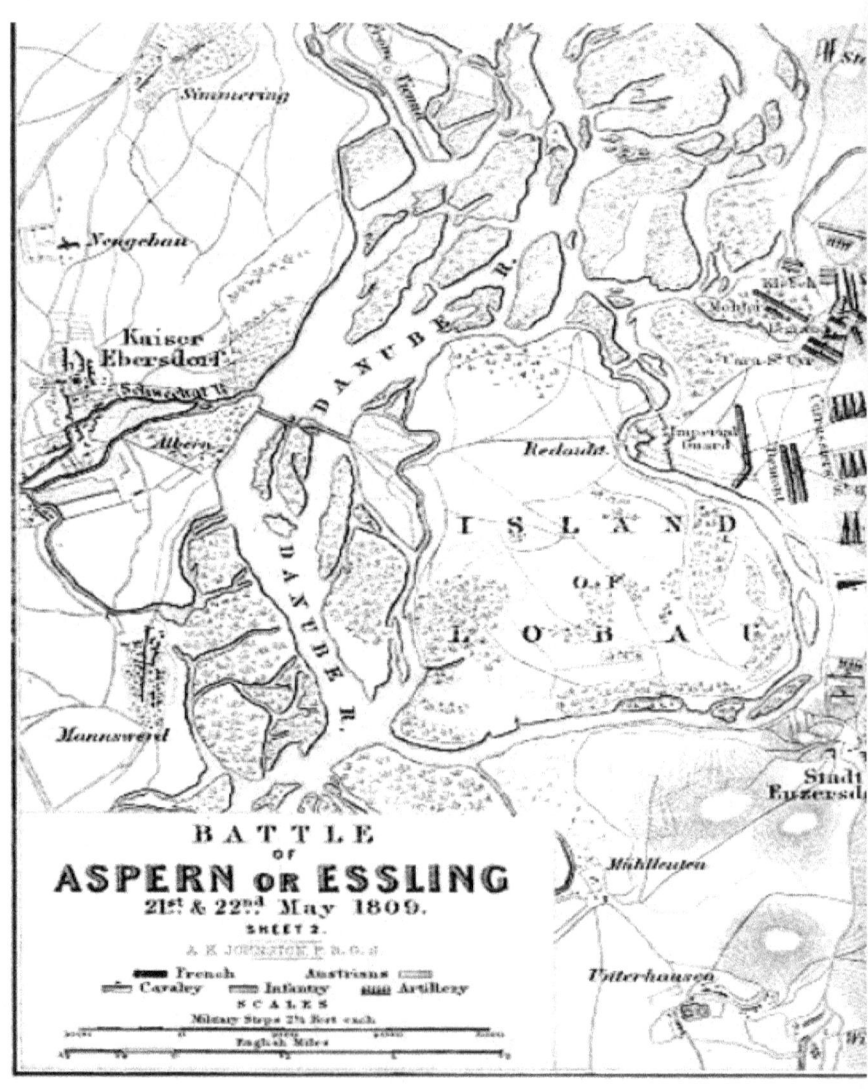

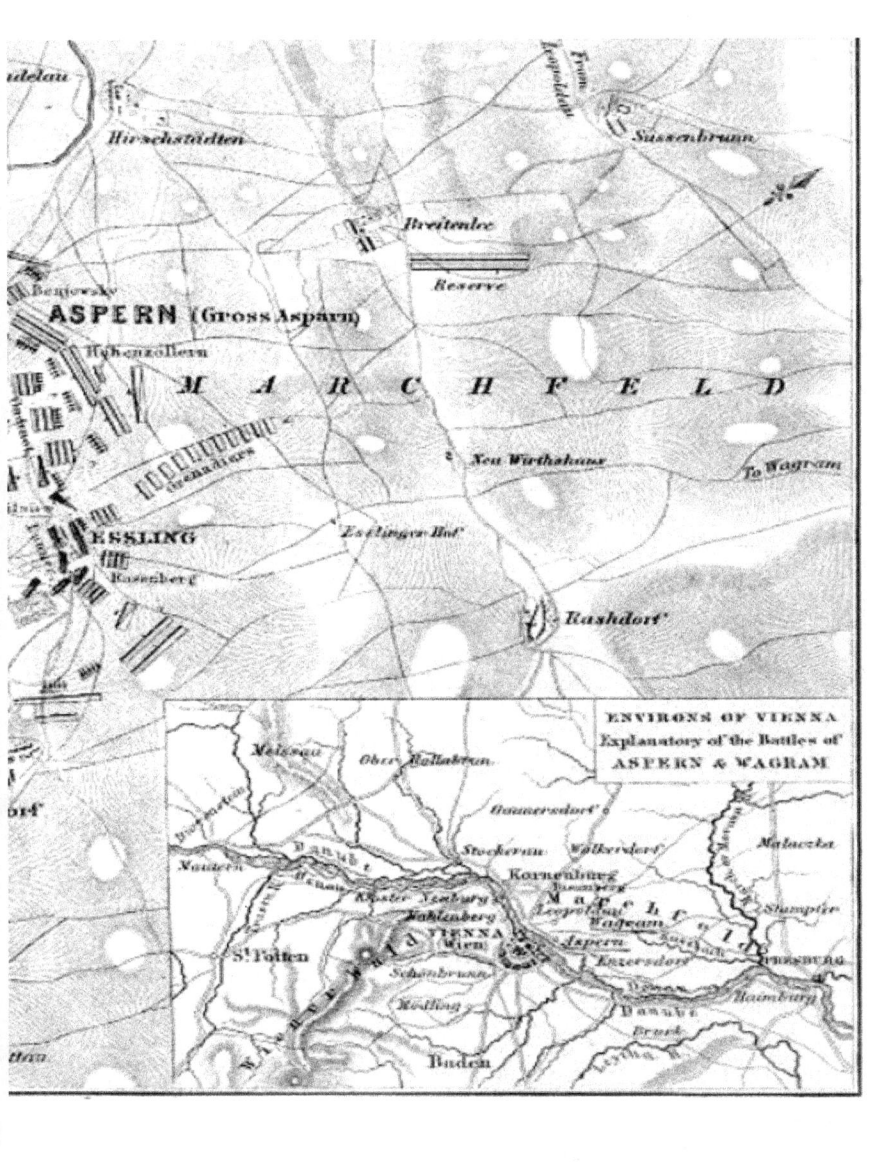

the 16th Chasseurs who were certainly part of his command, though directly under Piré and positioned at the outset facing towards the principal advance of the Austrians. Given Lasalle's character, it is not hard to imagine that he would not miss an opportunity to plunge into the fray. He also confirms that General Espagne was killed, in fact sabred to death, in one of these cavalry *mêlées*.

Thoumas also recounts an incident which concerns this point in the battle and it is included here in its entirety:

> Bessières, surrounded by Austrian *Uhlans*, after having seen his *aide-de-camp* fall beside him, fired his two pistols, and held his sword in his hand to defend himself. When Lasalle, whose lucidity at the thickest part of the fray, perceived the danger, which the marshal was in, he disengaged him by a suitably made charge, just as he had saved Davout in Egypt and Murat at Heilsberg.

Whether this incident occurred, the present writer is not in a position to confirm. As events go, one might imagine it would be significant enough to be a matter of common record, though this does not seem to be the case. Common sense tells one that any senior French officer (particularly one in command of the entire cavalry force on the battlefield) must have placed himself in a seriously perilous position to be described as 'surrounded' by enemy cavalry. Any individual armed only with a sword so closely pressed would indisputably be in serious trouble if those who surrounded him were numbers of enemy lancers (*Uhlans*) and that would apply to any single hussar riding to his rescue. Be that as it may, stranger things have, of course, happened. In fact, Bessières was fated to die in battle four years later near Lützen, despite his seniority, bizarrely killed instantly by a cannonball which hit a wall, rebounded off it and thus struck him full in the chest.

At 6.30 p.m. the bridge of boats broke yet again with its inevitable consequences. The fading light did not break off the collision between the armies and at 8 p.m. Lasalle's cavalry was still in

Lasalle at the charge

action throwing back Austrian attacks. At 10 p.m. the bridge was repaired again and, once more, French troops were able to cross the Danube to shore up the manpower in Napoleon's dwindling defensive perimeters. During the night the bridge broke again as a result of Austrian fire and it was not repaired and operational again until sunrise of the second day of battle.

Dawn came at about 4 a.m. and the battle raged once more. By 8 p.m. the French infantry was advancing into the attack and Lasalle, together with massed light and heavy cavalry, was ordered to support this effort. Bessières was then ordered to charge the Austrian batteries and Lasalle's command in company with that of Marulaz managed to not only overrun the guns but charge on and through ranks of enemy infantry. Predictably, the Austrian infantry formed for defence, the light cavalry was unable to break them and before long Austrian cavalry arrived on the scene and drove the French horsemen back. It might be said the cuirassiers had slightly more success, but eventually the outcome was the same. Thoumas reports that he has evidence based on eye-witnesses of Lasalle during this period, which would suggest that the man was in his element.

Meanwhile, the Austrian had prepared and set adrift a huge makeshift fire-ship on the Danube which fulfilled its task brilliantly by crashing into the bridge and breaching it effectively again. This was the pivotal moment. Lannes' attack had faltered and the Emperor came to the conclusion the battle could not be won so ordered the army to retreat slowly towards the ditch. A long day of bitter fighting followed as the French, cut off from reinforcements and supply, fought a defensive battle to hold their enclave from utter ruin. Aspern and Essling villages were scenes of carnage. Lannes was fatally wounded by a cannonball, removed from the field and died nine days later. Aspern was lost and Essling was probably only in French hands by default. For Napoleon, the imperative was now to save his army by moving them back onto Lobau.

Deprived of all hope of victory, the cavalry devoted themselves to the safety of the army, and by repeated charges slowed

The Wounding of Lannes at the Battle of Essling

down as much as possible the advance of the Austrians. When the army had retreated to the bank of the river, the archduke ceased to actively pursue it, for his army had also been badly mauled. The final stage of the battle was confined to a violent cannonade with massed Austrian pieces, arranged in a semi-circle, directed a converging fire upon the French, to which their half-demolished artillery could do little in reply, having by this time no more ammunition than a few grapeshot which had been reserved for the case of a final assault attempt by the Austrians. Lasalle's cavalry stood behind the artillery and remained motionless beneath this murderous fire. During the two days of the Battle of Aspern-Essling, it lost nearly half its strength.

21. The Battle of Wagram, 5th and 6th July, 1809

After Aspern-Essling the Austrian Archduke Charles pulled his army back a few miles to the north to Wagram to receive reinforcements and supplies. Now no longer under the imperatives of a battle in progress, Bertrand, Napoleon's chief engineer could properly construct a bridge fit for an army to cross the Danube. The work took two weeks to complete and when it was operational, Lasalle was sent across it with his division and placed under the orders of Davout. From the Battle of Aspern-Essling to the Battle of Wagram, he ceaselessly patrolled the country between Vienna and Pressburg (present day Bratislava).

Montbrun, meanwhile, who commanded the 2nd Light Cavalry Division of the Cavalry Reserve, had been sent with this division to the Army of Italy under Eugène de Beauharnais, where he took part in the battle and siege of Raab. Thoumas has Lasalle present at the investment, collaborating with Lauriston, combined with references to Lasalle's extraordinary achievement concerning the capitulation at Stettin by guile, which the present writer has elected to treat with some caution after examination of the contemporary understanding of facts concerning the Raab action.

Napoleon spent a month and a half turning Lobau into an impregnable base of operations. He brought Eugène to his side from Raab, Marmont from Dalmatia and Bernadotte from Linz, raising his numbers to 180,000 men and 750 guns. The Austrians, entrenched between Aspern and Essling had 140,000 men

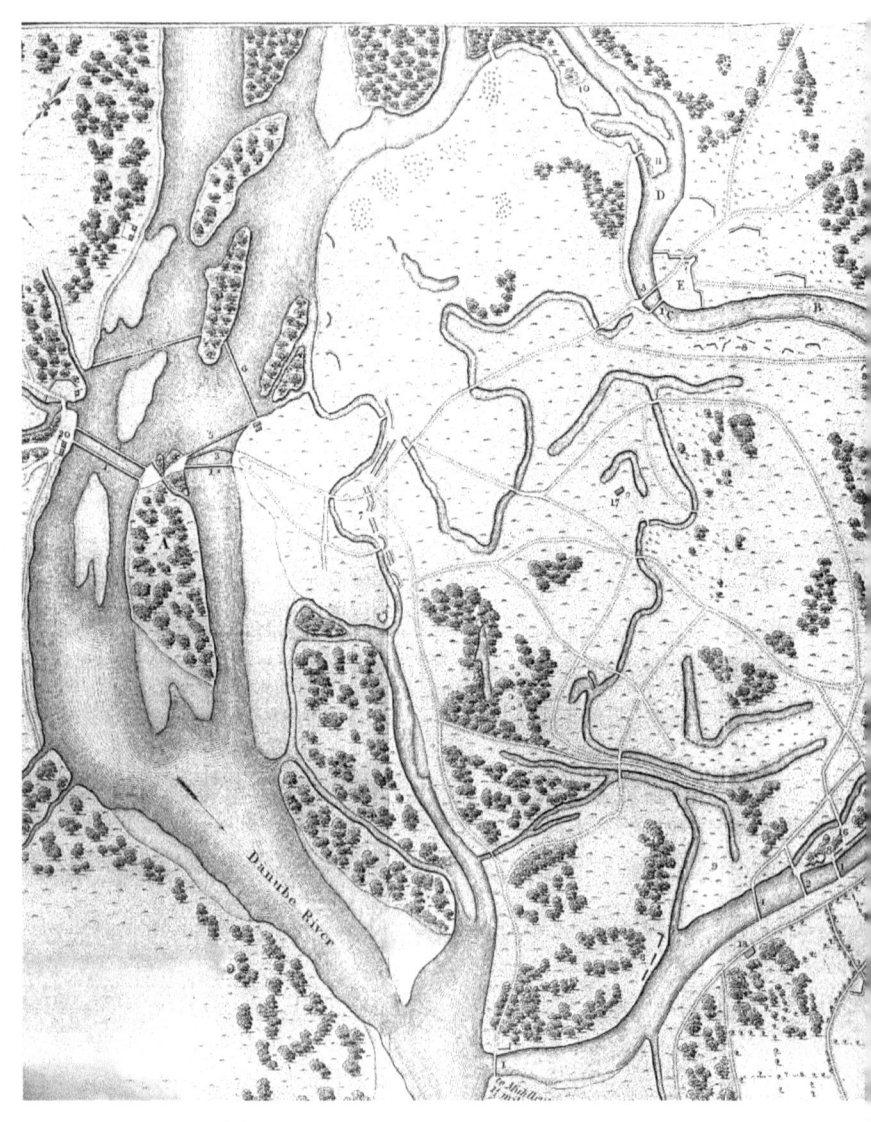

The island of Lobau

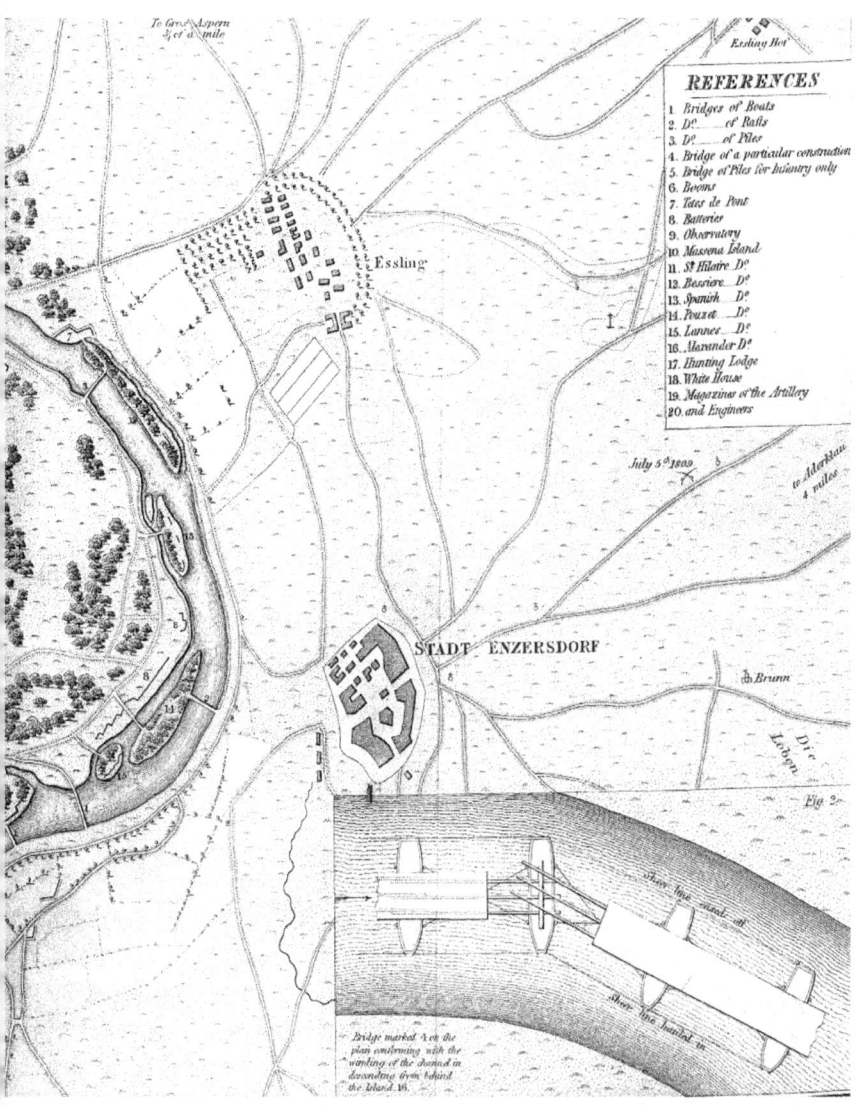

WITH FIELDWORKS

The Battle of Wagram, 1809

and 700 guns, excluding the 30,000 troops under Archduke John at Pressburg.

On July 1st the division under Legrand crossed the river from Lobau in a feint at the original crossing point, thus turning the Austrians attention from activities taking place on the eastern side of the island.

Lasalle was recalled to the island of Lobau and again crossed the Danube on the stormy night of the 4th to 5th July. By all accounts Lasalle was his usual self: radiant with pleasure at being once more upon the field of conflict and full of pride at being at the head of his fine cavalry division. It was now up to strength following the losses it had suffered in May and recovered from the fatigues of constant patrolling along the valley of the Danube.

The crossing from the eastern end of the island effectively turned the works of Archduke Charles. At daybreak the Archduke was astonished to see the French Army deployed in the Marchfeld on their left at Enzersdorf. He at once evacuated his trenches and took up new positions, which extended a full 15 miles. Napoleon assaulted on the right, centre and left essentially turning the battle into an uncharacteristic and unimaginative pounding contest. The French held a salient against the Austrian re-entrant and at 7 p.m. an unsuccessful attempt was made upon the heights of Russbach.

Of the cavalry, with which we are particularly concerned, the division of Montbrun together with that of Grouchy had been placed to the right under the orders of Davout. Lasalle was placed under the command of Masséna, on the left, with the light cavalry of Marulaz.

On the following day, July 6th, the Austrians took the offensive. The archduke's plan was to hold with his left, crush the French left with his own right and cut Napoleons connection to Lobau, then move into the assault with his left to destroy the enemy. For his part, Napoleons objective was the plateau of Wagram, the possession of which would enable him to outflank the Austrian left. This task was assigned to Davout. Masséna was moved to Aderklaa and two divisions (Boudet and Legrand) consisting of 18,000 men would protect Aspern and the Lobau bridges.

The archduke hammered at Boudet and Legrand but, Masséna carried out the retrograde movement intended to cover the outlet of the bridges. The French centre held firm, Davout and Grouchy appeared on the heights of Neusiedel and Oudinot appeared on Wagram. At this point, confident of success, the emperor, it has to be acknowledged with no little aplomb, snatched a few minutes sleep. He then launched Macdonald with a column of 8,000 men at the Austrian centre. By the time it reached its objective this column had suffered enormous losses, but the Young Guard was thrown forward in support. The Austrian army was cut in two. Masséna marched to advance and at 3 p.m. the archduke, knowing he was beaten, ordered the retreat.

Wagram was principally an affair of guns and infantry. Lasalle and Marulaz with the cavalry, with little real work to do themselves, were charged with protecting the flanks of the infantry so it could do its work. The Austrian cavalry, superior in number, repeatedly forced them back briskly several times, but the French cavalry stuck doggedly to its protective role.

This, as may be understood, was not the kind of action that sits well with the cavalry. So, it was fatally in the evening, after the signal to advance, which had been impatiently expected was at last given to the whole line, Lasalle, who had for several hours gnawed at the restraints imposed upon him was able to order an attack. Released from immobility he threw himself and his men (who were heavy cavalry—*cuirassiers* of the 1st Regiment) upon the retreating enemy with more enthusiasm and less prudence than the situation called for.

> 'He plunged through several "squares", tumbled the Austrian line in front of Leopoldau,' writes Thoumas, 'and, still at the head of his division, fell suddenly struck with a bullet at the front. His soldiers, who worshipped him, furious at his death, avenged him by slashing everything they found before them.'

Lasalle at Wagram with the 1st Cuirassiers

Once again it seems churlish at the point of Lasalle's final charge to glory to question whether he plunged through several squares (or *battalionmasse* in this case) since many a cavalryman has come to destruction attempting to break into just one infantry square, for their purpose is designed precisely to counter the success of such an act as the French cavalry had experienced most recently to its cost at Aspern-Essling. The present writer is minded of an incident at the Battle of Aliwal, 1846 where a mounted sergeant of the British Army's 16th Lancers cried out to his comrades, 'Here's to death or a commission' and pressed into a square (triangle) of Sikh infantry only to fall moments latter pierced several times by bayonets and shot. Infantrymen of the age of musket and cavalry everywhere knew well a square broken by cavalry meant ruin.

Lasalle's terms of duty bears the mention: 'killed by a cannonball,' but as most students of the period know this is an error. Lasalle, after a last charge against Klenau's corps, sounded the rally when a wounded Austrian infantryman (others say 'a retiring Hungarian grenadier'), who was fifteen paces from him, fired his weapon at him and lodged a bullet between Lasalle's eyes. Unusually, the stricken man was not killed instantly and was carried to Schöenbrunn, where he died two hours later. (This is the account of General Watier, junior? then a *sous-lieutenant* and witness to the event).

Lasalle's good friend, Paul Thiébault took the news of his friend very much to heart.

> 'Alas!' he lamented, 'when the terrible bulletin of the Battle of Wagram reached me, it brought me the first, but also the last news which I was to receive of poor Lasalle since our leave taking. He had died a hero's death, leaving to me a grief, which will only terminate with the end of my own life. Yet that loss, no less irreparable for France than for me, was rendered still sadder by other losses less harrowing but still sad enough. Pouzet, whom I had seen so brilliant on the field of Austerlitz, had similarly paid with his blood for the laurels gathered amid the chances of that

struggle; the worthy Saint-Hilaire had not survived it; and, lastly, Gautier, whom I loved next to Lasalle, and who in respect of eminence and of valour was in the first rank of the warriors that France ever possessed, completed the sum of three who made that day for me a day of bloodshed and mourning; and what tells a tale of incredible injustice is, that that officer, fit as he was to do honour to the marshal's baton, died a general of brigade, after holding that rank for eight years, to the disgrace of those to whom the disgrace is due.'

It is worth noting that Thiébault seems to speak of Aspern-Essling, in which Pouzet and Saint-Hilaire were killed, as if it was one and the same battle as Wagram, in which Gautier and Lasalle fell. It looks as if the indisputable defeat of Aspern-Essling had, from Thiébault's perspective, been kept dark till it could be reported together with the victory of Wagram, which took place some six weeks after the first engagement in the valley of the Danube.

★★★★★★

Pierre Charles Pouzet volunteered to join the French Army in 1781. By 1793 he was a lieutenant and mentor to the young Jean Lannes, with whom he maintained a lifelong friendship. By 1809 Pouzet was commanding a brigade in Saint-Hilaire's division. On the second day of Aspern-Essling he was standing in conversation with Lannes when he was struck by a cannonball which decapitated him. It was this event, which prompted Lannes to move to the position where minutes afterwards he also was mortally wounded by a cannonball. Pouzet's commander in the battle was Louis-Vincent-Joseph le Blond, Comte de Saint-Hilaire. From an aristocratic family, Saint-Hilaire had been a soldier since he was fifteen years old. By 1809 he was in his forty second year and a general of division. He was mortally wounded by a cannonball which ripped off his left leg.

Nicolas Hyacinthe Gautier (who was originally and in-

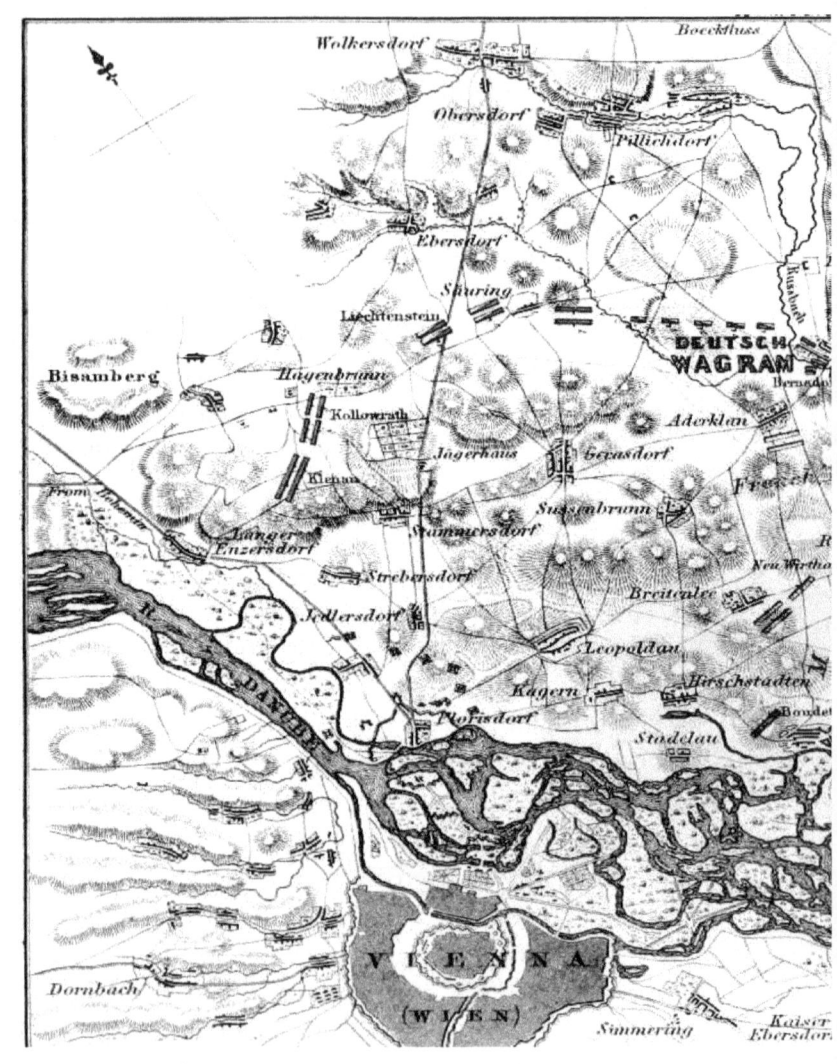

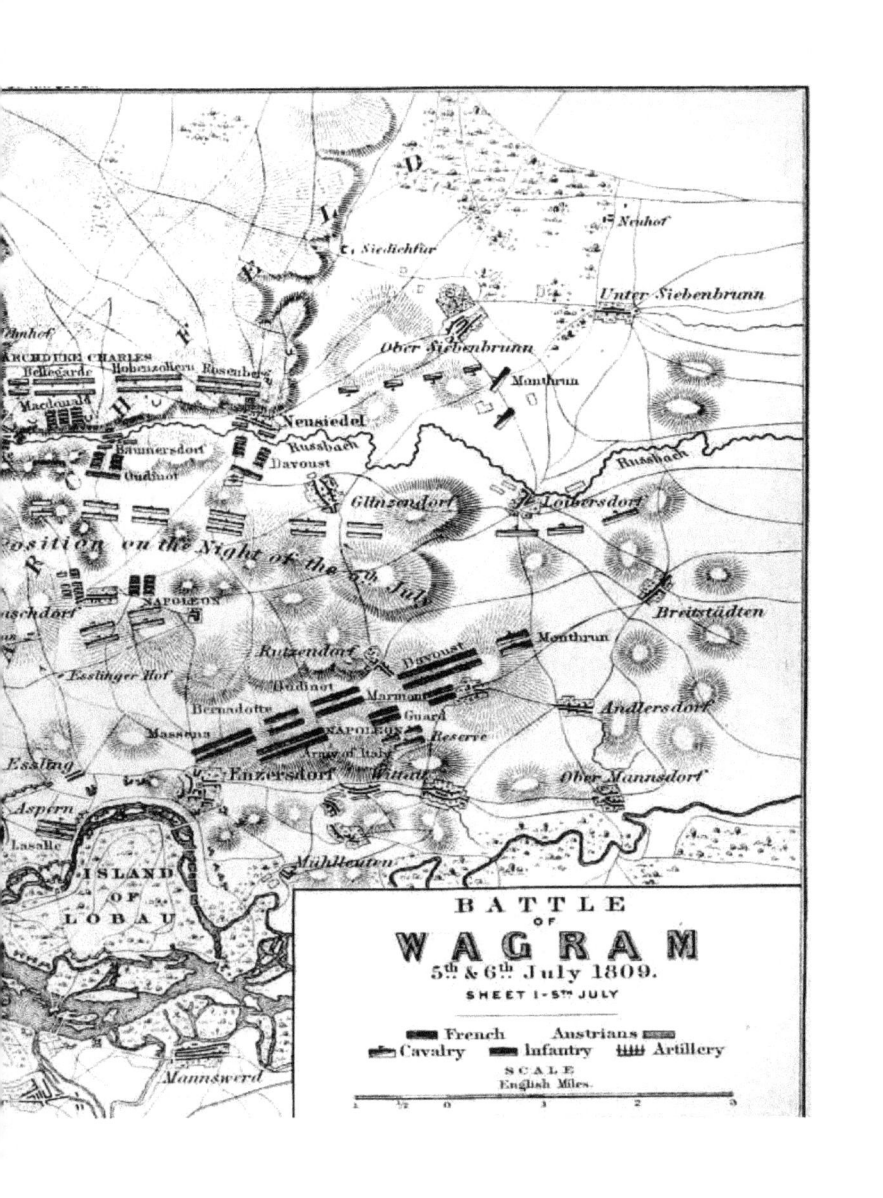

correctly cited as 'Gauthier' in the Thiébault memoir) had been an officer in the French Army since 1792. He became general of brigade in 1805, contrary to Thiébault's view, commanding the 2nd brigade of Gudin's division though he had been nominated Chief of Brigade at a point that corresponds to Thiébault's recollections.

In 1808 Gautier was made a Baron of the Empire. After Cervoni was killed at Eckmühl, he became chief of staff to Lannes. After Lannes was killed, Gautier became chief of staff to Oudinot. Gautier was then mortally wounded himself at Wagram. It is fair to note that, for a soldier who had served with distinction from the days of the armies of the Revolution, Gautier's progress in promotion does seem painfully slow, even to arrive at general of brigade, compared to that of several of his peers.

The campaign on the Danube of 1809, irrespective of the loss in senior officers, had proved to be a particularly costly affair for the French. The Austrian losses at Aspern-Essling and Wagram were similar in numbers to those of the French though, significantly, Austria was just one of the nations allied against France at this time.

★★★★★★

General Roguet in his *Souvenirs Militaires* says:

> Lasalle, one of our best generals of light cavalry, charged the Austrians who were in retreat beyond Leopoldau. He was riding forward in his usual impulsive manner when a bullet struck him in the forehead. During so many days when his sharp eye was useful he had been seen in the midst of his fellows of general rank and his colonels when suddenly he would leave the bowl of punch around which he grouped them all, take horseback to charge about the battlefield, where he never lost sight of any incident. Beloved, admired by all, brilliant, active, his resolutions were as sudden as they were happy.
>
> Lasalle did not usually suffer, according to Thoumas, from the

presentiments of sudden death that have been reported to have disturbed the final hours of certain men on the eve of battle. In fact, Lasalle does not appear to have been concerned with the prospect of an early death occasioned by falling in battle to any degree. When he was crossing Spain (as has already been recounted) he visited his friend, General Thiébault in Burgos on April 29, 1809. During a well-documented supper, Lasalle was reported to have said:

> Why spare my life? I've lived enough now. Why does one want to live? It is to make one's fortune and to make one's way. I am thirty-three years of age, I am a general of division, and the Emperor has given me an income of fifty thousand *francs* a year.

At this point, not unreasonably, one of his interlocutors pointed out to him that one had to continue to live to enjoy all the advantages he had acquired. Lasalle replied:

> No! That is not the case. We enjoy our lives in the acquisition of all these things. We enjoy making war and it is already a pleasure sufficiently great that in the of making the war one is within the noise, smoke and movement of battle. Then when one has made a name for one's self, well, one has enjoyed the pleasure of doing so. When one has made a fortune, one can be confident that one's wife and children will be wanting for nothing. All of this is enough for me. I can die tomorrow! (*Souvenir de Roederer*).

The above notwithstanding, it is said that on the eve of Wagram Lasalle may have had an idea of his approaching death. It has been reported (though the present writer cannot verify the source) that when Lasalle opened his baggage before Wagram he discovered that his pipe, a bottle from his cellar and the glass covering the portrait of his wife were broken. Taking this as an ill omen he confided in his *aide-de-camp* Du Coëtlosquet that he did not expect to survive the forthcoming battle. As with so many Lasalle anecdotes this is an appealing one.

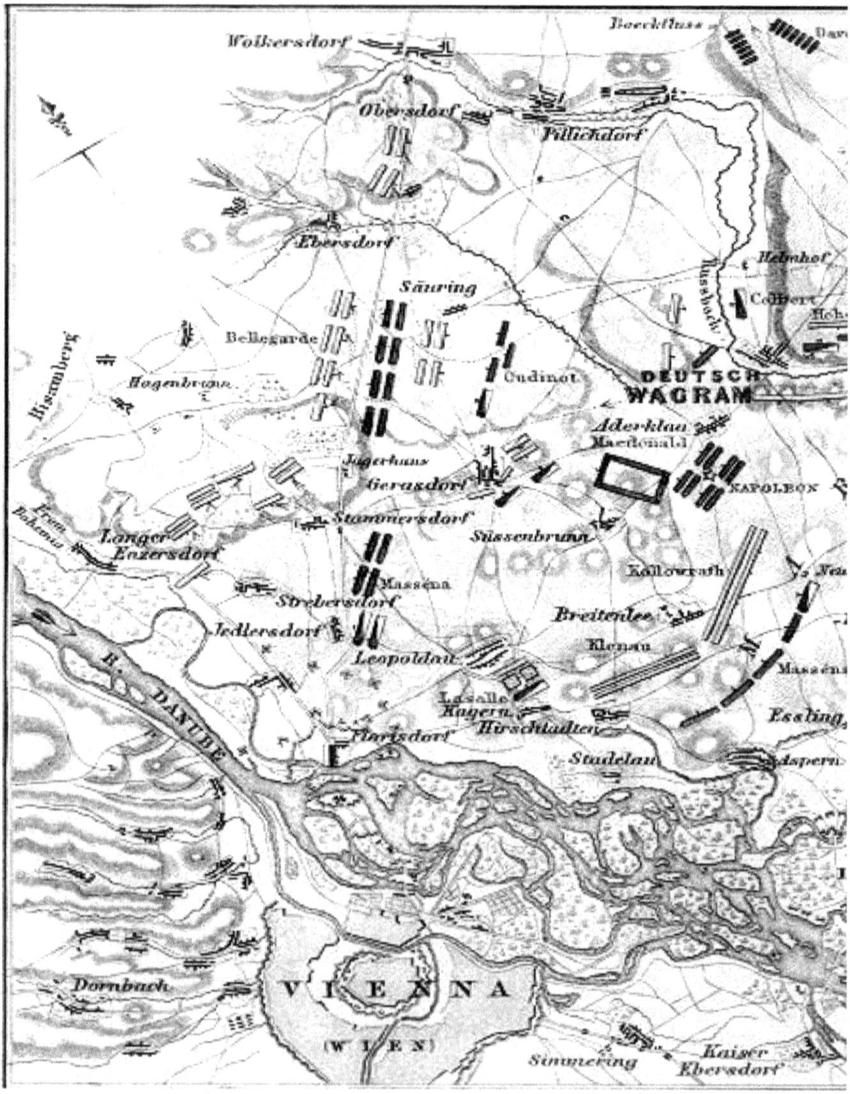
Wolkersdorf
Boeckfluss
Obersdorf
Pillichdorf
Ebersdorf
Säuring
Bellegarde
Bisamberg
Hogenbrunn
Oudinot
Russbach
Colbert
DEUTSCH
WAGRAM
Aderklaa
Macdonald
NAPOLEON
Jägerhaus
Gerasdorf
Stammersdorf
Süssenbrunn
From Bohemia
Langer Enzersdorf
Kollowrath
Massena
Strebersdorf
Breitenlee
Jedlersdorf
Klenau
Leopoldau
R. DANUBE
Lasalle
Kagern
Hirschtädten
Stadelau
Essling
Dornbach
VIENNA
(WIEN)
Simmering
Kaiser Ebersdorf

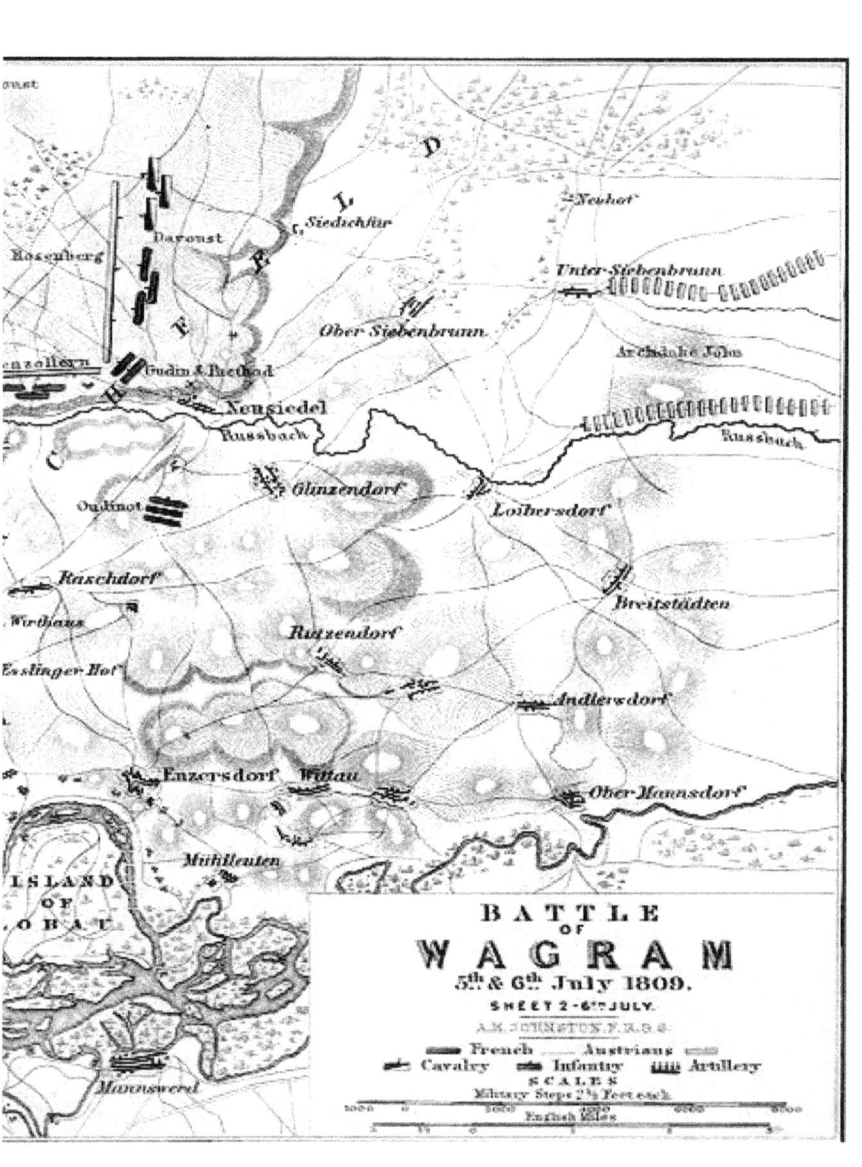

Lasalle's wife and child

However, more practically and verified, Lasalle having but one legitimate daughter and not wishing to see his name extinguished, solicited from the emperor (through the intervention of the statesman and diplomat, the Duc de Bassano, Hugues-Bernard Maret) the authorisation for the sons of the first marriage of his wife to adopt his name. This authorisation was granted, and the name of Lasalle was preserved under that of Berthier de Lasalle.

Lasalle's daughter, Joséphine Charlotte, born 1806, became in due course Madame la Countess Yermeloff and had two daughters, Mmes de Podenas and de Champeaux. Michel Yermeloff was a Russian Major-General (1826) and *aide-de-camp* to the Grand Duke Michael Pavlovich. He eventually settled in Paris with his wife.

Irrespective of the circumstances these provisions were not unreasonable on the part of a soldier who lived his life in the heat of battle, much less one who made clear that nothing in his life was more important to him than his profession.

22. Lasalle Assessed by His Peers

As for the military value of Lasalle, it is undisputed since he was one of the finest commanders of cavalry of his time. By that measure of the man, few of his peers were in disagreement. After having recounted the Battle of Wagram, Marmont expressed himself thus in his own *Mémoires*:

> The battle was won and the enemy in full retreat. The last of our cavalry charges made upon him at the commencement of his retrograde movement, cost us one of our finest officers, the much distinguished, General Lasalle, one of our companions from Italy and Egypt, a man endowed with a keen eye, with an admirable military instinct and great vigour.

Marmont once again, in his work *Institutions Militaires*, proposed that only three officers of the French Army, during twenty-five years of war of his time, were able to effectively lead and control the masses of cavalry and these were Kellermann, Montbrun and Lasalle. General Foy, speaking of the men who were 'in the habit of regularising the vast hurricanes of the cavalry of the age' also quotes just four names: Murat, Lasalle, Kellermann, and Montbrun.

Writing in the early 1870's when the cavalry arm was still an essential component of every army, Thoumas wrote:

> It is now fashionable to distinguish two classes of generals of cavalry. The first is skilful in illuminating the army and in tracking down the enemy. Of this type we may recall the famous portrait of Stengel, traced in Napoleon's

Mémoires on the campaign of Italy. This was a commander of cavalry skilled, intelligent and alert. A man able to recognise parades, fords, provide guides, interview mayors, parish priests, link intelligences with the inhabitants, find and use spies, seize and analyse letters and point towards subsistence for the army which follows them. The second class, realising in combat the ideal described by General de Brack, concentrate on a correctness of feeling, the rapidity and haughtiness of the glance, the promptitude of determination and action, the momentum, the firmness, *sang-froid,* that is essential for the cavalry.

He concludes:

According to certain military writers, including the most distinguished, Lasalle would be, with Stengel, demonstrative of the most perfect representation of the first type. Montbrun and Murat would have personalities of the second type. However, it would be a singular recognition of the services rendered by Montbrun in the campaign of 1809 that he should not be placed at the forefront of the vanguard generals as it would be that Lasalle based on his performances at Rivoli, Rio-Seco, Medellin, Aspern-Essling, could not be regarded as an off-line battle general.

In his full career Lasalle did little upon active service for which history may reproach him as regards his abilities as a soldier and commander of soldiers in the field. He may have been blamed, for the first time in 1806, by Napoleon, for having allowed himself to be played at Weissensee by Blücher, but on balance the reproach was unworthy and unjust.

A second time Lasalle was demonstrably at fault was in 1809, would be by the judgement of Masséna, for not having recognised the presence of the Austrian Army in the Marchfeld plain on the eve of the Battle of Aspern-Essling. This may be the only serious fault he committed. In fairness to Lasalle, he merely expressed an opinion to Masséna on the eve of Aspern-Essling. His superior knew well that none of Lasalle's patrols had been able

GENERAL LASALLE

to penetrate the dense Austrian cavalry screen to provide definitive information. In the event Aspern-Essling was a battle fought by the French 'with the cards they had been dealt' in consequence of the repeatedly failing bridge across the Danube and that had nothing to do with Lasalle's actions. Had Napoleon any choice in the matter or fore-knowledge, that battle would not have been fought at all. In fact, blame here surely rests entirely with the emperor, ever the chancer, for hastily moving parts of the army across the river in the face of a numerically superior enemy army upon an unreliable bridge.

> Lasalle (opines Thoumas) was an excellent general of the advanced guard, unflagging, especially in pursuit. On the field of battle, he possessed in the highest degree, the qualities of a master of his craft, the keen eye of observation, the promptitude of resolution, the impetus and vigour of decisive action.

General Foy appears to have been in accord with this view, for he wrote that Lasalle:

> Possessed a faster glance and a flash of determination more suddenly than the galloping courier, vigour, youth, good eyes, a resounding voice, the address of an athlete and the agility of a centaur.

Thoumas wrote:

> It would, moreover, be unjust to regard Lasalle as a brave and vigorous sabre, and prodigal in all circumstances of the blood of his soldiers.

He then gave his readers a quotation from one of the soldiers who served under Lasalle in the 10th Hussars.

> 'When Lasalle was named Colonel of the 10th Hussars,' said an old captain of the Empire in 1826 to the young officers who listened eagerly to him, each one of them was in the regiment: 'Here is a *sabreur* (swordsman) who will make us flee on the first occasion; Soon, it was astonishing

to find in him the most savage leader of the blood of his soldiers: for instance, when one had to give a neck-strap, no one gave him more vigorously, and knew better than to carry off his people.' (M. de Colbert, *Traditions et Souvenirs*, 3rd vol. M. de Colbert had been in 1816 an officer in the same regiment as this old captain, M. Robaly.)

I have retained the above quotation as it translates into English directly from the French in Thoumas text for the sake of interest. Readers will appreciate the quote takes unravelling as to its meaning. How I read this is as follows:

The appointment of Lasalle to the 10th Hussars meant that the regiment was getting a new commanding officer, about which the rank and file knew little as regarded his professional competence for the role. They did know of Lasalle's reputation, but as primarily, given their suspicion it seems, as a dandy and libertine. They doubted he was a 'real' soldier and the use of '*sabreur*' is intended cynically. Would Lasalle have so little substance that he would be unreliable on the battlefield and 'flee' *i.e.* not close with the enemy ordering a retreat thus disgracing the regiment? However, surprisingly to themselves, it became clear Lasalle was a real leader—a 'soldiers soldier'. The vigorous use of the 'neck-strap' here is used as a cavalry metaphor since the application this part of the harness can be employed sharply by the rider to achieve direct results. So the old soldier's view was that Lasalle was able to make immediate battlefield decisions and give effective orders to ensure his troops under his command were handled to the best effect.

Curély's manuscript, always sober of praise, reads:

Lasalle was one of the bravest of the French Army, had a good instinct, and was careful, if necessary.

Given the reliability of Curély, perhaps we may assume he implies, 'was careful *when he thought* it was necessary.' There is evidence enough for us to judge how often that was.

23. Marbot's Assessment of Lasalle

The substantial published memoirs of Jean Baptiste Antoine Marcellin de Marbot are probably the most well-known French light cavalry officers' recollections of the Napoleonic period. Readers of this book, arriving at this point within it, will have appreciated that the 'type' of light cavalryman that Lasalle represented was in no way confined to him or, indeed, originated by him. Lasalle may have been an extreme example of the breed, but demonstrably he was not alone in that category, nor yet the most extreme example of it on record. What has brought fame to Lasalle is his success as a light cavalry officer of his time combined with typifying traits, which were they entirely absent from his personality would be more noteworthy than their presence.

Marbot's assessment of Lasalle after his death (perhaps predictably since it is in accord with the views of others of Lasalle's peers), combines his admiration for Lasalle the leader of cavalry with a note of censure as regards Lasalle's personal behaviour. Most particularly Marbot regrets that Lasalle influenced young officers to the degree that they were determined to emulate him in every respect, but who, ultimately lacking the innate talent to become a version of the total man became, instead, nothing more than poor examples of his very easily acquired vices. This made them less useful than an officer of mediocre abilities who might, at least, be reliable.

This is a reasonable view of the responsibilities of total leadership by understanding the necessity of presenting an example to subordinates, though it is not one that should readily trans-

General Jean Baptiste Antoine Marcellin de Marbot

pose perhaps, in its entirety into our understanding of what that might mean according to a modern moral compass. In fact, despite Marbot's assessment and opinions, most readers of Marbot's adventures would be justified in believing that Marbot was not so very far from the Lasalle model himself. It should also be noted that both these men, among others, were examples of what their master, the emperor, approved, encouraged and expected them to be.

Sir Arthur Conan Doyle's fictional French hussar, Brigadier Gerard, is estimated to be based on Marbot and certainly the basis of some of Marbot's exploits can be found in Gerard's adventures. Lasalle, perhaps unsurprisingly, also appears in the Gerard stories.

Doyle was widely read on the subject of the Napoleonic era and possessed a comprehensive library on the subject. So, it is certain that he had insights into what made the composite fictional light cavalryman of Napoleon's army and he undoubtedly found elements of that character in both Marbot and Lasalle. The Gerard stories, written for a British audience, portray their hero as a comic figure. From the perspective of the British public of their day Gerard's antics, despite his obvious courage, gelled with its preconceptions and prejudices of the stereotypical French soldier. In fact, were we to strip away just some of the humour resulting from the dim-wittedness that is an essential part of Brigadier Gerard's character, what remains, is a fairly accurate description of who these cavaliers of the First Empire of the French actually were in thoughts and deeds. An anecdote concerning Lasalle's wedding plans, according to Marbot demonstrates this perspective succinctly.

The following passage comes from Marbot's memoirs concerning Lasalle's career and is reproduced here in its entirety.

> General Lasalle, who fell at Wagram, was keenly regretted both by the Emperor and the army. He was the best light cavalry officer for outpost duty and had the surest eye. He could take in a whole district in a moment, and seldom made a mistake, so that his reports on the enemy's position

were clear and precise.

He was a handsome man, and of a bright wit, but, although well educated, he had adopted the fashion of posing as a swashbuckler. He might always be seen drinking, swearing, singing, smashing everything, and possessed by a passion for play. He was an excellent horseman, and brave to the point of rashness.

Although he had fought in the first revolutionary wars, he was little known before the famous campaign of 1796, when, as a captain in the 2nd Hussars (This is not quite accurate. Thoumas tells us Lasalle was a *chasseur* and was promoted to the 7th Hussars), he attracted the notice of General Bonaparte at the Battle of Rivoli. This took place, as is well known, on a lofty plateau bounded on one side by steep rocks, at the foot of which flows the Adige, along the road to Rivoli. The Austrians, having been beaten by the French infantry, were leaving the battlefield by every available way.

One of their columns hoped to escape by reaching the valley over the rocks; but Lasalle followed them down this difficult passage with two squadrons. In vain it was represented to him that cavalry cannot be employed on such dangerous ground. He galloped down the descent, followed by his hussars; the astonished enemy retreated headlong. Lasalle overtook them and made some thousand prisoners under the eyes of General Bonaparte and the army.

From this day onwards, Lasalle was in high favour with Bonaparte, who promoted him rapidly and took him to Egypt, where he made him colonel. In one of the numerous engagements with the Mamelukes the thong which held Lasalle's sabre to his wrist broke; he dismounted in the thickest of the *mêlée*, and, undisturbed by danger, picked up his weapon, nimbly remounted, and dashed at the enemy afresh. One must have seen a cavalry combat to appreciate the courage, coolness, and dexterity which such a deed requires, especially in presence of horsemen like the Mamelukes.

Lasalle had intimate relations with a French lady in high society, and while he was in Egypt their correspondence was seized by the English and insultingly published by order of the Government—an act which, even in England was blamed. A divorce followed, and on his return to Europe Lasalle married the lady.

As general, Lasalle was placed by the Emperor in command of the advanced guard of the Grand Army. He distinguished himself at Austerlitz and in Prussia; having the audacity to appear before Stettin and summon the place with two regiments of hussars. The governor lost his head and brought out the keys, instead of using them to lock the gates, in which case all the cavalry in Europe could not have taken it.

This feat brought Lasalle much credit and raised the Emperor's liking for him to a high point. Indeed, he petted him to an incredible degree, laughing at all his freaks, and never letting him pay his own debts. Just as he was on the point of marrying the lady to whom I have referred Napoleon had given him 200,000 *francs* out of his privy purse.

A week later, meeting him at the Tuileries, the Emperor asked, "When is the wedding?"

"As soon as I have got some money to furnish a home with, sire."

"Why, I gave you 200,000 *francs* last week!" exclaimed the astonished Napoleon, "What have you done with them?"

"Paid my debts with half and lost the other half at cards," replied Lasalle innocently.

Such an admission would have ruined any other general. The Emperor only laughed, and, merely giving a sharp tug to Lasalle's moustache, immediately ordered Duroc to give him another 200,000 *francs*.

At the close of the Battle of Wagram, Lasalle's division had

Senior officers of cavalry, 1809

not been engaged. He came and begged Masséna to let him pursue, and the marshal assented, on condition that he would act with prudence. Hardly had Lasalle started, when he saw a brigade of enemy's infantry, which was hastening, closely pressed, to reach the village of Leopoldau, in order to obtain a regular capitulation and escape the fury of the victors in the open.

Lasalle guessed what the Austrian general was after, and, pointing to the setting sun, addressed his men, "The battle is ending, and we alone have not contributed to the victory. Come on!"

He dashed forward, sword in hand, followed by his squadrons, and, in order to prevent the enemy from entering the village, made for the narrow space now left between the head of the column and Leopoldau. The others, seeing themselves cut off from the hoped-for shelter, halted and opened a brisk file-fire. A bullet struck Lasalle in the head, killing him on the spot. (It did not as it transpires, as has been explained. JHL) His division lost a hundred troopers, besides many wounded. The Austrians opened their way to the village, and when our infantry divisions came up, capitulated, the officers declaring that that had been their intention in making for Leopoldau.

Thus, Lasalle's charge was useless, and he paid dear for a mention in a bulletin. His death left a great gap in our light cavalry, which he had trained to a high degree of perfection. In other respects, however, he had done it much harm. The eccentricities of a popular and successful leader are always imitated, and his example was long mischievous to the light cavalry. A man did not think himself a *chasseur*, still less a hussar, if he did not model himself on Lasalle, and become, like him, a reckless, drinking, swearing rowdy. Many officers copied the fault of this famous outpost leader, but none of them attained to the merits which in him atoned for the faults.

The final paragraphs of Marbot's assessment of Lasalle are

without doubt a damning indictment of his behaviour, particularly during the last moments of his life. As regards the closing acts of the Battle of Wagram, it is clear that Marbot has given an accurate description of the events.

There can be little doubt that Lasalle behaved irresponsibly, recklessly and from a tactical perspective (an essential consideration for an officer of his rank) pointlessly.

Anyone who has read anything of the behaviour of cavalry on the battlefield throughout history knows that the men of the mounted arm were often the bane of an army commander's life because their sole purpose and desire was to engage in a charge and that blinded them (officers and men alike) once their 'blood was hot' to all consequences. Ensuing events regularly resulted in disaster. This chapter might be henceforth filled with examples taken throughout the centuries, but there is little doubt that most readers of this book could readily bring examples to mind with very little effort or assistance.

Marbot clearly admired Lasalle professionally, however he recognised that at Wagram Lasalle did not just effectively kill himself, but that he needlessly spent the lives of his men in an attempt to slaughter an enemy body of troops that was not just fleeing, but that was certainly in the assessment of all concerned, simply positioning itself away from open ground so it might more safely surrender.

Reprehensible though that may be, particularly by some modern standards, we cannot ignore this insight into an element of Lasalle's character, for this once again demonstrates that he was a ruthless and dangerous man compelled, once he had allowed himself to surrender to his baser instincts and subordinate his considerable intellect, to enter in acts of violence for the sheer exhilaration and joy they brought him, thoughtless of any other consideration. Of course, to be fair to the man, there was little guile about him (except when he was applying it to others in the field) and he was on record as admitting as much without feeling any need to excuse himself.

Unfortunately, for Lasalle at Wagram, his defeated prey on

this occasion still had some bite left to it and he paid the price of his impetuosity. It seems that Marbot's principal issue is that Lasalle's action immaturely, irresponsibly and selfishly deprived the army of his nation the value of his demonstrable talents and on the basis of the evidence it is, perhaps, difficult to disagree with him.

The Statue of Lasalle at the Château of Lunéville
Note cavalry horse in the background

24. The Hussar General Commemorated, 1809-1893

The Napoleonic era has, for several reasons, endured in the public memory, largely undiminished by the two centuries or so that have elapsed since it finally fell to the allied armies after the Waterloo Campaign in 1815. Despite having much against its credit, history and popular recollection has largely been positive as regards the days of the First Empire of the French. The period has many aficionados among those who study history. It is not difficult to understand why this is the case. The Napoleonic era possessed the appearance of exuberant and romantic glamour, which encompassed every aspect of its being, with the exception of the carnage of the wars it instigated during which, it is estimated, up to 6,500,000 civilians and military personnel lost their lives.

Towering over this entire epoch is the monumental figure of the man whose name it bears. Possessed of several of the often dubious credentials that qualify a human being for greatness Napoleon Bonaparte stands in the first rank. He has left his mark upon the history of the world in memory and in practices, many of which endure to this day. In central Paris, the French capital, his works and deeds are omnipresent, for despite a popular revisionism concerning Napoleon, particularly as regards the imperial period, references to the man and his times remain commemorated indelibly everywhere in the city and are impossible to ignore or avoid. Indeed, even farther afield, Napoleon, his works and battles have become nothing less than a tourist industry of some considerable value and proportions. This is, it has to be acknowledged, in some contrast to the fates of several despots whose monuments and names have been systematically eradicated from the cities of their home nations.

Without Napoleon there could not have been a Lasalle as we know him, just as there could not have been most of the outstanding figures in the ranks of the *Grande Armée*, for Napoleon formed those times and crafted the lives of those who lived under his pervading influence. Lasalle was, in the final analysis, simply one of Napoleon's many outstanding lieutenants: A larger than life figure who was also a fine general of light cavalry, which was an arm that displayed military costume at its most extravagant and encouraged among its men deeds, which would justify the definition of 'cavalier'.

No one may say what the future may have held for Lasalle had his renowned 'luck' not deserted him at Wagram. There were many battles fought by Napoleon's France after Lasalle's death and his talents and propensities would have dictated he would have fought in all those that came his way (and no doubt in some he had to find for himself) in the saddle, like Murat, in the heart of the danger.

Had he survived to the end of the imperial age, however likely or otherwise that might have been, there can be little doubt Lasalle would have become an even more universally renowned as a leader of mounted troops. Had age and experience tempered his personal behaviour one can readily believe a marshals baton would have been within his grasp for as a light cavalry commander he had few, if any, equals alive during his time and none that arose thereafter.

Certainly, Lasalle was in no position to have prevented Napoleon's fall and it is difficult to imagine a place for Lasalle after Napoleon, for if the age of Napoleon defined Lasalle then he personified that age with every fibre of his being. Perhaps, like the fictional Brigadier Gerard, he would have become old and sad with only a glass of wine and his memories for company. However, as Lasalle made clear; he had made 'provision' to ensure that would never be his fate and destiny may always be given a nudge of assistance.

So Lasalle rode out of life as he had ridden through it and it is impossible to imagine—given the evidence to the contrary—he would have conceivably wished it otherwise for men like Lasalle do not, as a rule, die in their beds of ripe old age. There is little value in judging him for misguided rashness or a failure of judgement that cost him his life, for to do so would imply that in that moment he was acting temporarily out of character, when nothing that he had done in his entire life would suggest that was the case.

Thoumas asked his readers, 'Have the honours, which have been indisputably rendered to Lasalle been worthy of his valour and reputation?' The answer was for most of the 19th century, for obvious reasons, that they had not.

Lasalle was an exceptional soldier in a time of great soldiers who were led by one of the most able soldiers that has ever lived. Had the First Empire of the French endured, this would be a question unworthy of the asking, because the power that made him and which he faithfully served would have ensured his perpetuated recognition. It was not to be, not least because Lasalle was a soldier fighting on the losing side and all that regarded him had less than six years to exist before its demise and replacement by the rule of the ancient order, which was an implacable enemy. Time moves quickly onwards and those who are not immediately commemorated are soon left behind in the mists of history as new as more relevant heroes rise to meet new challenges in the causes of the governments of their nations.

According to the Thoumas' text, Lasalle's body did not rest in the country of his birth. His remains were buried in Austria in the great cemetery of Vienna, a dozen miles from the place where the fatal bullet struck him, within a tomb constructed by order of his family. In 1891 Lasalle's remains were repatriated to Les Invalides in Paris. Rue de General Lasalle was named in his honour in Paris in the 19th arrondissement in 1894. Several military and educational buildings also now bear his name.

We will find his name in France inscribed upon the walls of the *Arc de Triomphe*, one of the most iconic landmarks, which stand in Paris, on the north-east side. This triumphal arch commissioned in 1806 after the victory at Austerlitz immortalises the outstanding military figures of the Revolutionary and First Empire periods. Inscribed upon its walls are 660 names of which 558 are the names of generals of the Napoleonic age. So, whilst that of Lasalle here does not stand apart, it may be fairly claimed that, upon the arch his recognition is in company with his finest peers.

A bust of Lasalle featured, before the conflagration of the Tuileries in 1871 caused by the arson of the Communards during the Paris revolutionary risings, in the Salon of the Marshals. After the fire Lasalle's bust was discovered intact amid the rubble of the palace, removed and placed in the galleries of Versailles.

According to an imperial decree of the 9th of February, 1810, a statue of Lasalle was planned to be ultimately placed in company with the statues of seven other prominent soldiers who had fallen on the battlefields of the empire. These were Espagne, (killed at Aspern-Essling, 1809), Saint-Hilaire, (mortally wounded at Aspern-Essling, 1809), Auguste Colbert ,(killed at Cacabelos, 1809), Ruffin, (mortally wounded at Barrosa, 1811), Lapisse, (mortally wounded at Talavera, 1809), Cervoni (killed at Eckmühl, 1809), and Hervo, (killed near Eckmühl, 1809). Together these statues would stand on the Concorde Bridge (Pont de la Concorde) crossing the River Seine in the heart of Paris.

This marble statue of Lasalle, according to Thoumas, was near to completion at the fall of the Empire. The powers of the Bourbon Restoration (which understandably had its own quite different ideas as to whose statues might rightly adorn this bridge) returned Lasalle's statue to storage where it remained until the creation of the Historical Museum of Versailles. It was then originally used to decorate the great courtyard of the palace.

Later this statue was once again moved and Thoumas reports sardonically:

He is one of those who seem to make a procession towards the statue of Louis XIV. and guard the arbours of the garden. However, this statue no longer has Lasalle's correct body as that body was used to support the head of Marshal Jean Lannes, whose name is inscribed on its pedestal. Frugal in its magnificence, King Louis-Philippe's government, gave France its great men at reduced prices.

The statue of Auguste Colbert, executed under the same decree as that of Lasalle, and destined as it also was to appear on the Concorde bridge, served instead as a body for the head of the statue of Marshal Mortier. In the same way, the statue of Saint-Hilaire, became a Marshal Masséna. The statue of Espagne, was transformed into some other unspecified personage.

Thoumas informs us:

> A young woman, the daughter of this general, summoned to attend the inauguration of her father's statue, found herself ill at the sight of this profanation, and nearly died of her destruction. (*Traditions et Souvenirs, 3e vol notes.*)

Thoumas wrote in protest:

> So many of our finest generals have been deprived of the honour decreed for them by Napoleon and their images consigned to obscurity. Many of them have been commemorated, but their busts, portraits and even their statues have been concealed behind the closed doors of the Museum of Versailles. Was it not fitting that Lasalle deserved to be glorified and a statue of this epitome of the cavalryman should rise in a public square or in a cavalry garrison town such as Nancy or Lunéville, for example?

In fact, today both a bust and a statue of Lasalle are kept at Versailles. Another modest statue of him stands in the Rue de Rivoli in Paris in a niche above the street where, in a line with the statues of many other highly regarded soldiers of Napoleon, he gazes down on the passing traffic.

However, perhaps to the satisfaction of all (especially including Charles Thoumas who unfortunately died in 1893 and so may have been unaware his wishes had come to fruition), a magnificent equestrian statue of Lasalle, the dashing hussar, as a General of Division was commissioned and sculpted by Charles Cordier in 1893. This statue embodies Lasalle as a man of action for blade drawn and mounted on a rearing, spirited war-horse eager for the charge he stands (or rather eternally rides) in the heart of the *château* of Lunéville, just fifty or so miles south of Metz, his birth place.

This is a fine statue and nothing less than that due to the memory of its subject as an outstanding soldier of France. Although Charles Cordier created some other equestrian statues, he is principally known for his beautiful busts of ethnographic subjects which demonstrate skill, artistry and a sensitivity, which reveals the essence of his models of the highest order. So far as the appointment of a sculptor is concerned, the memory of Lasalle could not, at the time, have been placed in better hands. Cordier's work may now been seen, incidentally, in the Musée d'Orsay in Paris.

This book began with a question which concerned the influence Lasalle had on the cavalry men of his own time. The age of the warhorse has now passed and cavalrymen now ride in battle tanks. However, the full colour cover of the French periodical, '*Le Petit Journal*' in the edition of the 7th of December, 1913 depicts the statue of Lasalle at Lunéville surrounded by French cavalrymen from many regiments, each with his sword raised in a salute towards the figure of the great horseman. The outbreak of the Great War, 1914-18 was just months in the future and Lasalle's death at Wagram, at that point, more than a century in the past. Nevertheless, it is apparent that Lasalle had remained undiminished in the hearts and minds of those who might justifiably have felt an affinity with him.

So, it would be a disservice to Lasalle to suggest that one should remember a man of great spirit solely as he is memorialised in monumental form, all be it the vibrant, animated work of a master, for whilst the flame of his life may have burned briefly, he lived it headlong—a true hussar—in the manner he chose and he ensured his flame burned brightly.

'*À moi, hussards!*'

FIN

STATUETTE DE LASALLE

Appendix

BRITISH INFANTRY IN SQUARE AGAINST FRENCH CAVALRY DURING THE PENINSULAR WAR

It was of course a very different matter when the French cavalry had to face the steady battalions of the British Army. Looking down all the record of battles and skirmishes from 1808 down to 1814, I can only remember two occasions when the enemy's cavalry really achieved a notable tactical success. Oddly enough both fell within the month of May, 1811. At Albuera there occurred that complete disaster to a British infantry brigade which has already been described in the preceding chapter. The other, and much smaller, success achieved by French cavalry over British infantry at Fuentes de Oñoro, a few days before the greater disaster at Albuera, has also been alluded to. These two disasters were wholly exceptional; usually the British infantry held its own, unless it was absolutely taken by surprise, and this even when attacked frontally by cavalry while it was deployed in the two deep line, without forming square. If the British had their flanks covered, they were perfectly safe, and turned back any charge with ease.

Indeed, the repulse of cavalry by British troops in line, who did not take the trouble to form square because their flanks were covered, was not infrequent in the Peninsular War. The classic instance is that of the 5th Northumberland Fusiliers at El Bodon in 1811, who advanced in line firing against two French cavalry regiments and drove them off the heights, being able to do so because they had a squadron or two of British horse to protect them from being turned. A very similar feat was performed by the 52nd at Sabugal in 1811: and Harvey's Portuguese brigade did as much at Albuera.

Much more, of course, was the square impregnable. When once safely placed in that formation, British troops habitually not only withstood cavalry charges at a standstill but made long movements over a battlefield inundated by the hostile cavalry. At Fuentes de Oñoro the Light Division, three British and two Portuguese squares, retreated at leisure for *two miles* while beset by four brigades of French cavalry, and reached the ground which they had been ordered to take up with a total loss of one killed and thirty-four wounded. Similarly, at El Bodon the square composed of the 5th and 77th retreated for six miles, in the face of two cavalry brigades which could never break into them. (For details see the chapter dealing with General Picton.) Indeed, it may be stated, as a rule almost without exception, that troops in square, whether British or French, were never broken during the Peninsular War even by very desperate and gallant charges. One of the best instances of this general rule was the case of the combat of Barquilla, where two grenadier companies of the French 22nd, surprised while covering a foraging party by five squadrons of British cavalry, got away in a level country after having been charged successively by three squadrons of the 1st Hussars of the German Legion, the 16th and the 14th Light Dragoons. One of these three squadron-charges, at least (that of the 14th), had been pushed home so handsomely that an officer and nine men fell actually among the French front rank, and a French observer noted bayonets broken, and musket barrels deeply cut into by the sweeping blows of the light dragoons, who yet failed entirely to break in. There was indeed only one extraordinary case of properly formed squares being broken during the whole war, a case as exceptional in one way as the disaster to Colborne's brigade at Albuera was in the other. This was at the combat of Garcia Hernandez, on the morning after the Battle of Salamanca, where the heavy dragoons of the K.G.L. delivered what Foy (the French historian of the war) called the best charge that he had ever seen. The rear-guard of Marmont's army had been formed of the one division which had not been seriously engaged in the battle, so that it could not be said to have been composed of shaken or demoralised troops. Nevertheless, two of its squares were actually broken by the legionary dragoons, though drawn up without haste or hurry on a hillside favourable for defensive action.

According to Beamish's *History of the German Legion*, a work composed a few years later from the testimony of eye-witnesses, the first square was broken by a mortally wounded horse, carrying a dead rider, leaping right upon the kneeling front rank of the square, and bearing down half a dozen men by its struggles and kicking. An officer, Captain Gleichen, spurred his horse into the gap thus created, his men followed, a wedge was thrust into the square, and it broke up, the large majority of the men surrendering. The second square, belonging to the same regiment, the 6th Léger, was a little higher up the hillside than the first: it was a witness of the destruction of the sister-battalion, and seems to have been shaken by the sight: at any rate, when assailed a few minutes later by another squadron of the German dragoons, it gave a rather wild though destructive volley, and wavered at the moment of receiving the attack, bulging in at the first charge. This was, of course, fatal. The broken squares lost 1400 prisoners, beside some 200 killed and wounded. The victorious dragoons paid a fairly high price for their success, losing 4 officers and 50 men killed, and 2 officers, and 60 men wounded out of 700 present; the extraordinary proportion of killed to wounded, 54 to 62 marking the deadly effect of musketry at the closest possible quarters. (Charles Oman, *Wellington's Army* illustrated edition published 2018 by Leonaur.)